# TORCH BIBLE COMMENTARIES

### General Editors

**THE REV. JOHN MARSH, D.PHIL.**
*Principal of Mansfield College, Oxford*

**THE REV. CANON ALAN RICHARDSON, D.D.**
*Professor of Christian Theology in the University of Nottingham*

# FOREWORD TO SERIES

The aim of this series of commentaries on books of the Bible is to provide the general reader with the soundest possible assistance in understanding the message of each book considered as a whole and as a part of the Bible.

The findings and views of modern critical scholarship on the text of the Bible have been taken fully into account; but we have asked the writers to remember that the Bible is more than a quarry for the practice of erudition; that it contains the message of the living God.

We hope that intelligent people of varying interests will find that these commentaries, while not ignoring the surface difficulties, are able to concentrate the mind on the essential Gospel contained in the various books of the Bible.

Volumes in the series include

# GENESIS 12–50

*Introduction and Commentary*

*by*

## A. S. HERBERT

*Professor of Old Testament Literature and Religion
in the Selly Oak Colleges*

SCM PRESS LTD
BLOOMSBURY STREET LONDON

FIRST PUBLISHED 1962

© SCM PRESS LTD 1962

PRINTED IN GREAT BRITAIN BY
NORTHUMBERLAND PRESS LIMITED
GATESHEAD ON TYNE

# CONTENTS

*Chapter and
Verse*

# PREFACE

The aim of this volume is to provide an exegetical and theological commentary on Genesis 12-50; it is based, as is usual in this series, on the Authorized Version (AV), although frequent reference has been made to the Revised Version (RV) and the American Revised Standard Version (RSV), and the alternative translations offered in the margins of these versions (m). Many important textual and literary questions have had to take a subordinate place in this study, although they have not been ignored. The valuable introduction to *Genesis I-XI* by Professor Alan Richardson in this series has, deliberately, not been repeated; it would be unnecessary to do so, and it may fairly be assumed that that commentary will have been studied.

These stories of the patriarchs are an essential part of Holy Scripture, the inspired and authoritative revelation of God, given to his people that they may know him and walk in his ways. That cannot be proved by argument, although there is nothing irrational in this belief. Neither is it to be proved, though it is often illuminated, by the success or failure to find archaeological points of contact with the narratives. Such methods would reduce the book to the level of merely human documents and records. But it can be tested in life. That, in fact, is what has happened in the long history of Ancient Israel and the Church. Genesis is a living book; its words have power to judge and to lead men into the life with God. Yet it is written in a language and against a background that is not ours. Both language and thought-forms must be translated so that the twentieth-century reader may share in, and be strengthened by, the faith of the people of God. This is what compels the long and patient work of Biblical scholarship to continue.

The author of this commentary is indebted to many, both living and dead, in the preparation of this volume; he would acknowledge his debt especially to Dr H. Wheeler Robinson who first led him into the paths of Old Testament Study, and who introduced him into the Society for Old Testament Study. For the fellowship and stimulus of this Society, no words of thanks can ever be adequate. The stimulus and encouragement of colleagues and students in the Selly Oak Colleges have contributed much to this commentary; for her help at every stage in the preparation of this book, the author would express gratitude to his wife.

# BIBLIOGRAPHY

S. R. Driver, *The Book of Genesis*, Westminster Commentaries, Methuen, London, 9th edition, 1913.

J. Skinner, *Genesis*, International Critical Commentary, T. and T. Clark, Edinburgh, 1910.

W. H. Bennett, *Genesis*, The Century Bible, T. C. and E. C. Jack, Edinburgh, (n.d.).

S. H. Hooke, *In the Beginning*, The Clarendon Bible Old Testament, Vol. VI, Oxford, 1947.

B. Vawter, *A Path through Genesis*, Sheed and Ward, London, 1955.

C. T. Fritsch, *Genesis*, Layman's Bible Commentaries, John Knox Press, Richmond, Virginia, 1959, and SCM Press, London, 1960.

G. von Rad, *Genesis*, Old Testament Library, SCM Press, London, and Westminster Press, Philadelphia, 1961.

G. E. Wright, *Biblical Archaeology*, Westminster, Philadelphia and G. Duckworth, London, 1957.

The Commentary is based, as requested, on the Authorized Version (AV) but, where necessary, corrections have been made. The Revised Version (RV) and Revised Standard Version (RSV) have been consulted throughout. Occasionally translations have been offered which depend on the best recent scholarship available to the commentator.

# GENERAL INTRODUCTION

' In the beginning God created . . .' These words belong not only to the opening chapter of Genesis but dominate the whole book, and furnish the clue by which we may understand much that is described in the books that follow. It is convenient to recognize that chapter 12 marks a division in the book, the beginning of the history of the patriarchs, or the story of ' the Founding Fathers '[1]; yet the real interest in Genesis 12-50 is not in the activities and fortunes of the patriarchs, but in the God of Abraham, Isaac and Jacob, the Lord who declared himself to Moses and guided the Israelites into Canaan. From this point the purpose of God becomes articulate as, in the nature of the case, it could not be in creation of the world and of mankind. We read this book in order that we may understand in its real depth that complex of events that we call the Exodus and Entry into the promised Land, i.e. God's call to and salvation of Israel, and the culmination of the divine purpose in the work of Christ. Genesis is not merely the first book in the Bible; it is the beginning of the history of salvation.

Obvious though that statement may be, it needs to be said, lest in discussion of the innumerable points of interest in these chapters the all-important fact may be overlooked. We may have an entirely proper interest in the literary phenomena displayed in the Pentateuch[2] or in archaeological discoveries which enable us to see a little more clearly the living background of the patriarchal period; or in a historical inquiry into the period from Abraham to the settlement in Egypt. But this book is not just a literary

[1] G. E. Wright, *Biblical Archaeology*, Westminster, Philadelphia and G. Duckworth, London, 1957, p. 40.

[2] Cf. A. Richardson, *Genesis I-XI*, Torch Bible Commentaries, SCM Press, London, 1953, pp. 13 ff.

production, or a source book of ancient history, and it was not the purpose of the writer(s) to satisfy those interests. The real interest is in what God was doing, and what was the manner of his rule. Furthermore that was a practical interest, since as these stories are told men may learn what is his will, and what are the consequences of loyalty and disloyalty in the ongoing life of his people, Israel. There were occasions in the life of Israel during the monarchy and during the Exile when men needed to be challenged in the midst of complacency or despair, to penitence or renewed trust. In such circumstances these ancient stories took on new depth of meaning. For it is the nature of God's dealings with men that they are never merely of the past; they belong also to the present and the future. Here, as elsewhere in the Bible, we are reminded that religion as understood by Jew and Christian is not based upon man's ideas about God, not even upon the teaching of enlightened saint or philosopher, but upon what God has done in the life and experiences of men. So we read of the divine call and promise, with implications far beyond the imagination of those who first received them; of men's faith and lack of faith, obedience and disobedience; and of God's control of events brought about by men's loyalty or failure, in order that his purpose may be accomplished.

These chapters will tell us of what God was doing through the fathers, for the creation and maintenance of his people's life through the generations that are to follow. But this in turn suggests the work of the inspired interpreters, those who shall read the signs of the times. Just as the scientist observes natural phenomena and, by reason of his scientific training, interprets them as the working out of the fundamental laws of nature, so the inspired teachers of Israel learned to recognize what God was doing and interpreted these events for the life of Israel. We may not know, for lack of evidence, precisely who first told or wrote these stories of Genesis, though we can sometimes detect the circumstances in which they received their present form. But we can recognize what manner of men they were. They were men who were devoted to the people of God and to the God who called this people into being; they were thus able to respond to the inspiration of God and to declare his purpose for the judgment and renewal of his people's life. To these men of God and their purpose we must now give attention.

## THE SOURCES OF GENESIS

Consideration has already been given in the earlier volume in this series to a study of the literary phenomena of the book that has led to a separating out of earlier documents, usually distinguished by the letters J, E, P. It seems probable that J, the Southern Kingdom tradition (Judah) was beginning to assume a fixed form in or soon after the Solomonic era, i.e. from about 950 BC; while E, the Northern Kingdom document (Ephraim) would find an appropriate setting in the period 850-750 BC. P (the Priestly material) comes from the Exilic period or early in the Persian period, i.e. about 500 BC and often appears to be making deliberate comment on the already known work of J and E. It should be noted that it is not always possible with certainty to distinguish between J and E; but a useful criterion is the interest shown in events connected with Southern and Northern shrines respectively. The Priestly material may be recognized by its interest in cultic practices, e.g. circumcision and in genealogies, and by its careful reiteration of the divine blessing and promise (cf. Gen. 17).

Two further points should be noted: (a) The relatively late date which the P material suggests does not mean that the earlier material is obsolete from the point of view of the final compilation of Genesis. Rather is the earlier material confirmed in its effectiveness by its inclusion. It had proved its worth in the life of the people of God, never more effectively than in the perplexing circumstances of the Exile. We can almost hear the guardians of Israel's faith saying: 'We did not fully listen to this in earlier generations and therefore this tragedy has befallen us. But God has not finished with us. And in that faith we will hear these traditions again in order to prepare ourselves for what he will yet do.' They are saying in their way what the prophets of the Exile were saying (cf. Isa. 51.1 ff.). The recognition of the Priestly document, *and the use it makes of earlier traditions* in the circumstances of the Exile is a clear indication almost amounting to proof that this material is divinely inspired, the work of the Spirit judging and renewing the life of man. (*b*) Concerning the documents themselves, whatever may be the exact date and circumstances in which they were written, it has always been recognized that they draw on much more ancient material, preserved apparently in oral tradition. Here it should be remembered that in the days before printing, and before reading and writing were commonplace activities of daily life, verbal memory was much more considerable and accurate than it is in an urban population today. We recall that the teaching of Jesus was thus faithfully transmitted in the life of the Church for at least thirty years before it was written down. Further, the spoken word has a directness and a vividness that the written word rarely retains. It is accompanied by change of tone, by gestures, the animated face of the speaker; it is more personal and more living. This we can test for ourselves. To listen to the Scriptures read well and with understanding is to enter more immediately into their meaning than to read them silently to oneself. This is even more true of the original language of the Old Testament, Hebrew, than of English, for Hebrew is essentially an oral rather than a literary medium of communication. So this written material in Genesis rests on even more ancient oral tradition. But who were responsible for remembering these stories? For what purpose and to whom were they recited? The answer is not explicitly given in the Bible but there are clues which suggest the answer.

We have already noted the connection between some of these stories and the sanctuaries which played an important part in the life of Israel under the monarchy, e.g. Shechem, Bethel, Hebron, Beer-Sheba. We know that an essential function of the shrine guardians was to teach the divine requirements to Israel as on various occasions—and especially on the great feast days—the people came to the sanctuary (cf. Deut. 33.10). It is evident that an essential part of the observance of sacred days was the question and answer whereby each generation was instructed in the faith (cf. Ex. 12.26 f.; 13.14; Deut. 6.20 ff.; 32.7; Ps. 44.1; 78.3 ff.). The Christian Church has followed this tradition in its catechetical and homiletic instruction and in its repetition of the Creed. At this point we may notice such credal material in the Old Testament as Deut. 26.5-9; Josh. 24.2-13; Ps. 105, and the prayer in Neh. 9.6 ff. In all these passages there is a recital of the saving acts of God whereby Israel became the Lord's people. They provide the living situation in the life of the worshipping community for these chapters of Genesis. They are not so much providing information about Abraham, Isaac and Jacob, as presenting the well known traditions in a distinctive way. Their aim is clear. It is to say what God was doing. They form the deposit of the teaching of faithful shrine priests (Levites) as it was given over the generations to Israel at worship. We know from the prophetic condemnations that many of these priests were corrupt and obscured the distinctive character of Israel's faith. The same condemnation is made against most of the prophets. But the books of the Law provide evidence that some, however small a minority, remained faithful to their ancient calling. When a prophet in his distress feels that he is alone in his loyalty, he is reminded of seven thousand who are still loyal to him who brought them out of bondage (I Kings 18.18). It is reasonable to suppose that they were built up in the faith through the medium of such teaching as we find in Genesis.

*The Character of the Patriarchal stories.* When therefore we read this book we are brought into the fellowship of a people at worship and receiving instruction in the faith, from the early days of Israel's life, through the times of general apostasy, in the dark days of national disaster and the hopelessness of the Exile, and during that difficult period of re-adjustment as they sought to be the people of God under alien domination, Persian, Greek and Roman. Moreover, it is clear that this material continued to be so used in the early Christian Church which knew itself, for all its predominantly Gentile character, to be the spiritual heirs to Abraham, Isaac and Jacob (cf. Rom. 4.3 ff.; Gal. 3.6 ff.; 4.28.). Now it is clear that these stories in Genesis are not offered to provide illustrations of good and saintly living, or of great heroism. Abraham, Isaac and Jacob are men of heroic stature; but they are not ideal figures. Some of the stories of the patriarchs present them in a very poor light even by their contemporary standards. (Romantic idealism is in fact remarkably absent from the Old Testament.) Evidently such stories were not the invention of a later age, but a making use of well-known material. We shall see in some of the accounts that customs and circumstances have been preserved that accord well with what is known from other sources of Canaan in the second millennium BC. But the ancient narratives have been used in a particular way for which perhaps the best descriptive word is ' parable ' as it is used in the Bible. That is, they are told in order to quicken awareness of God's active rule in human life, of his judgment and saving purpose even when men through lack of faith involve themselves in disaster. They will thus arouse men to penitence and renewed trust and obedience. In this sense it is undoubtedly true to say that the Patriarchal stories present in terms of individual lives the long discipline of Israel. They declare in this parabolic fashion the divine purpose for the people of his choice, and the sovereignty of God made manifest in their life. These chapters begin and continue with the account of God the Creator, who called men to serve him loyally and promised them the land. But even in their failure and sin this over-ruling and redemptive purpose is at work, as it is finely expressed at the end of the Joseph story 50.20.

## HISTORICAL BACKGROUND OF GENESIS 12-50

From various incidental references that appear in these chapters, and a correlation of these with recent archaeological study, the period of the patriarchs appears to fall into approximately the three hundred years from about 1650 BC. Abraham's immigration from Ur to Haran and thence into Canaan appears to be connected with the unsettled conditions brought about by the Amorite invasions of Mesopotamia and Northern Syria. A number of districts in this area came under Amorite rule, the best known being the state of Babylon, ruled over by Hammurabi 1728-1686 BC. Other states under Amorite rule were Mari and Haran. From excavations at these places information has been gained which bears on the customs encountered in the Genesis stories; while the names Abram, Jacob and Benjamin (as the name of a tribe at Mari) appear among the Amorites. Canaan was a land of city states whose princes were normally vassals of the Egyptian Pharaohs. It was apparently the Amorite peoples who invaded Egypt and ruled there as the Hyksos dynasty during the seventeenth century. But other great movements were taking place at this period, and in the seventeenth and sixteenth centuries the Hurrians (Biblical Horites), themselves under pressure from the Hittites, were invading Mesopotamia and Syria.

Egypt eventually threw off the yoke of the Asiatic Hyksos
dynasty after a century of domination, and re-established
after a struggle its control over Canaan, but it is evident
from the Biblical references that pockets of the various
invaders remained in the land after the various tides of
invasion had receded, and apparently retained some of their
own customs. This new Egyptian kingdom (18th Dynasty)
lasted for over two centuries (1570-1310 BC) but its closing
years were a time of weakness, and it was unable to control
Canaan. For that land was liable to invasion, not only from
the 'great powers', but also from wandering bands of freebooters. During the reign of Amenophis IV (Ikhnaton),
Egypt was gravely weakened by internal dissension, pro-
voked by that Pharaoh's monotheistic (?) interests whereby
he came into conflict with the powerful priests of Amun,
high god of Egypt. The internal weakness of Egypt made it
possible for these freebooters to enter Canaan, and break
up the imposed unity of the peoples. The story is told in
the Amarna letters where we find reference to these wandering bands under the name of Khapiru (Apiru or Habiru).
While this name cannot be certainly equated with Hebrew,
and indeed the name appears elsewhere and at various
dates in Asia, it is at least possible that there is some connection between them and the account preserved in Genesis
34. Furthermore, the story of Joseph, a slave who rose
to high position, accords well with other references to these
peoples. The book of Genesis does not give us a continuous
story; the patriarchs do not appear by name in any contemporary records. But what is told is in general terms
appropriate to the conditions as we now know them from
the seventeenth to the fourteenth centuries BC.

## THE RELIGION OF THE PATRIARCHAL AGE

There are two aspects of this subject: (a) the religion of

the people in the land of Canaan; (b) the religion of the patriarchs themselves. While we may not draw sharp distinctions between these two aspects, there is evidently something distinctive about the latter, though this is seen rather in its effects than in any precise statement. A distinctive difference may be found in recognizing the religion of Canaan as being a nature religion whose deities, male and female, were expected to promote the fertility of flocks and crops. It is difficult to estimate how far the religion of the patriarchs as presented has been influenced by the faith of the post-Mosaic age, but at least it appears to be of a personal character, not exclusively related to the natural cycle, and claiming personal allegiance, trust and obedience. The full blaze of the burning bush has not confronted the patriarchs, but the God they worshipped, under whatever name, is recognizably the same as the Lord who 'heard the cry of affliction' from the land of Egypt. This is to recognize the revelation that came to Moses, and its continuity with what Israel's forbears knew.

The Old Testament makes a number of allusions to the kind of religion believed in and practised in Canaan; and it is clear that the religion of Yahweh, God of Israel, was engaged in a long struggle against these beliefs and practices. Our knowledge has been greatly extended by the discovery of a number of religious texts, relating to the cultus from Ugarit—the Ras Shamra texts. These, together with the investigation of many of the ancient sacred sites mentioned in the Bible, have given us a remarkably clear picture of Canaanite religion. We know of El (one of the words translated 'God' in EVV) and his consort Asherah (AV 'grove') and their son Baal Hadad, the god of rain and vegetation, and his consort Anath (she was still being worshipped by the Jews who had fled to Egypt as late as 400 BC). The great enemy of Baal was Mot (Death) who annually destroyed him and from whose kingdom Anath rescued him so that once more the life-giving rains might

come. Many other deities appear, each with his or her particular function, e.g. Dagan (OT Dagon) the corn god,
and Shalim (from whom Jerusalem received its name; cf. also
Solomon, Absalom), the god of health. To these deities
various rites were performed accompanied by the recital of
myths, designed to identify the activities of men with their
mysterious powers in the natural world. Since the main
interest of the people of Canaan was in agriculture, the
dominating thought was in the promotion of the fertility
and productivity of the land and the herds. It is for this
reason that the sexual activities of the gods are so prominent in the myths, and were imitatively performed by the
participants in the ritual. Gods, men and nature were bound
together in a unity. It was the aim of the ritual to maintain
that unity.

It is much more difficult to define at all precisely the religion of the patriarchs. It is obvious that a distinction must
be made, since it is virtually impossible to imagine the kind
of religion we find in Canaan having any continuity with
that of Moses. One of the reasons for our difficulty lies in
the fact that the patriarchal stories assumed their present
form in a later age, and all after the decisive revelation to
Moses. Inevitably that experience has affected the form
that the tradition has taken. We may note the way in which
the Jew and the Christian differ in their understanding of the
Old Testament. In the latter 'the law, the prophets and
the psalms speak' of Jesus Christ, and we can no more read
the Old Testament without the New than we can (with
understanding) read the New Testament without the Old.
Further, while one of the three main traditions (J) ascribes
a knowledge of the name YHWH to the patriarchs (cf. 15.8;
28.13 where the words GOD and LORD printed in capitals
correspond to the name), another (P) explicitly denies that
it was known before the time of Moses (Ex. 6.3) and the
third (E) does not in fact use this name in Genesis. Further,
our English translations somewhat obscure the occurrence

of various names for God in this book (cf. 14.18), some of which are known to have been used in Canaanite religion as personal names. Some writers have suggested that the patriarchs were monotheists. Such a view seems to the present writer impossible to maintain on the evidence provided and improbable on other grounds. Monotheism is a term appropriate rather to the religious philosopher than to Biblical religion. In any case there is nothing distinctively Biblical about monotheism; such interpretations of the nature of deity have arisen in various parts of the world. What is more important is to recognize the relationship which is described as existing between the patriarchs and God. It was thoroughly personal in character; it was based on the divine call and man's response. God and man are not bound together in a unity, but in a covenant. God claims from man an absolute allegiance and gives him a promise; man can only enter fully into this promise as he learns to trust and obey. We do not find the patriarchs sacrificing (as did the Canaanites) to secure the divine favour, or to cajole God; they sacrifice because God has come to them, and as a means whereby they may in gratitude give themselves to him. They may well have shared many of the beliefs and customs of their contemporaries; but in the kind of relationship depicted as brought about by God with man we find a distinctive religion which could, and did, bear the weight of the great revelation to Moses.

## CONTENTS

Gen. 12-50 may be divided into three main sections.

A. Incidents relating to Abraham 12–25.18.
B. Incidents relating to Jacob 25.19–36.43.
   (The only section relating exclusively to Isaac is Chapter 26 and this story is quite clearly a duplicate of the

similar story of Abraham 12.10–13.4; 20.1-18. Isaac is little more than a necessary link in the transmission of the Blessing and the Promise from Abraham to Jacob.)

C.    Incidents relating to Joseph 37-50.

Included in these chapters is an ancient tradition about Judah and his descendants which is not connected with the Joseph story, Chapter 38. It does however accord with other references in the Old Testament which suggests that the Judaean clans settled in the South independently of the other tribes. Also included is Jacob's blessing (49), more correctly a collection of blessings and curses.

# COMMENTARY

## A. ABRAHAM 12.1–25.18

### THE DEPARTURE OF ABRAM

#### 12.1-9

Apart from vv. 4b, 5 (P), the whole chapter comes from the J source. After the bare statement of immigration in 11.31 f. (P), the narrative takes on colour and depth. The point of departure is Haran in northern Mesopotamia in the district of Aram-Naharaim (Aram-of-the-Two-Rivers) cf. 24.10, or Padam-Aran (the Field of Aram) cf. 25.20, 28.2, etc. It lies between the upper reaches of the Tigris (Biblical, Hiddekel, Gen. 2.14; Dan. 10.4) and Euphrates.

The significance of this incident, as indeed of all Abram's life, is made clear in vv. 1-3. We are not told how the divine command came; but it was an absolute command, with the assurance of the divine blessing and requiring unreserved trust and obedience. No further explanation is given for Abram's departure other than this command. It is not suggested that he was a monotheist, or disgusted with contemporary polytheism. That is too intellectualized and rationalistic an explanation. The best comment is that of Heb. 11.8, 'when he was called . . . (he) obeyed.' That is the essential human element in the Biblical conception of revelation. But that obedience is itself the outcome of faith, and that is made clear in 12.1. We have been told that Abram had no child (11.30). Now he is to leave his country, clan and father's household; thus the assurance of blessing that follows must appear virtually impossible of achievement. This was a far more serious demand than it would be for man in a modern industrial society. It is not only the sundering of the ties of family love. <u>The father's house is the source of psychic life in which each member shares.</u> For a nomad to be out of the clan is to be without protection and safety. There is a strong emotional tone about this verse. Thus vv. 2 f. gives the divine blessing which shall take the place of the all-important father's blessing (cf. 27.27; 48.15).

The blessing is of great importance in the life of Israel. It was understood to convey the personal energy and quality of him who offered it, and to contain its own energy of fulfilment; he who was blessed received this energy into his own soul. So this divine blessing in 12.2 f. is a potent factor in Abram's life and in the life of his descendants. It is the apparent impossibility of realizing this blessing for lack of a son that underlies the episodes until the birth of Isaac (ch. 21) and gives meaning to the supreme test in ch. 22.

### 3. Curse . . . curseth

Two different Hebrew verbs are used here. The first suggests isolating a man from community with the living world so that he dies of exhaustion (cf. 3.14, 17; 4.11); the second means to make light of a man, i.e. deal with him as though the divine blessing were not in him (cf. Ex. 21.17). The same thought is expressed in Matt. 5.22. The refusal to recognize the plain fact of the divine activity cuts man off from the source of life, the living God. BE BLESSED. The form of the Hebrew verb here and at 18.18; 28.14 is ambiguous. It is properly a reflexive although it is used as a passive; hence RSV 'Bless themselves'. Another form, exclusively reflexive, is used at 22.18; 26.4, although AV translates this also as passive. Probably the reflexive meaning should be preserved in both sets of passages and the distinction we make may not have been so apparent to the Hebrew mind. For in 'blessing themselves', i.e. calling

upon themselves the divine gift to Abram, the nations
would manifest the beginning of faith as they perceived the
source of Abram's blessing. Thus they would enter into
relationship with God through Abram, and share in his
blessing.

### 6. Sichem
(Shechem), the modern Nablus, plays a considerable part
in later Israelite tradition. It was a sacred place of great
antiquity and appears to have had a particular importance
for Covenant making (Judg. 8.3; 9.4; Baal-berith means
'Lord of the Covenant'). PLAIN OF MOREH, more correctly
'Oak (RSV) or terebinth of Moreh'. Moreh means teacher
and the reference is to some well-known tree believed to
be animated with oracle giving-power, cf. 35.4.

### 7. 
cf. 13.15; 15.17, 18; 17.8. The frequent repetition of this
promise suggests that it belonged to some shrine liturgy in
the life of Israel (cf. Ps. 105.11).

### 8. Beth-el
i.e. House of El, another ancient sanctuary. Excavations
at this site indicate that in this period it was a prosperous
city. Two traditions in Gen. 28.19; 35.7, preserve the older
name of this sanctuary, Luz, and associate its renaming with
Jacob; a third, Judg. 1.23, associates its renaming with the
invasion of the Josephite clans. This renaming of an ancient
Canaanite sanctuary is a mark of Israelite possession.

### Hai
(Ai as in Josh. 8) was destroyed in 2,000 BC and was in
Abram's day, as the name suggests, a ruined city.

### 9. South
or the Negeb, appears to have been more fertile in the
second millennium BC and, though not capable of support-

ing a large population, was eminently suitable for semi-nomads.

## ABRAM IN EGYPT

### 12.10-20

Although this section preserved an old folk tradition, it is presented in such form as to insist that, contrary to Abram's expectation, the Lord was able to preserve the integrity of his people even in Egypt.

Egyptian tomb-paintings from 2,300 BC to 1,300 BC represent nomads entering Egypt in search of pasture. Normally they would be temporary residents, v. 10: TO SOJOURN THERE, though some of these immigrant groups might merge with the Egyptian population. The temporary character of Abram's migration is emphasized. Egypt is not the land of promise.

Various features of the story that follows may be noted. 1. A variant of this story appears at ch. 20 (E), though the place (Gerar in Canaan close to the Egyptian border) and the King (Abimelech) are different. A further variant occurs at 26.1-11 (J), but tells of Isaac and Rebekah, and Abimelech is described as King of the Philistines. It is evident that this is a story preserved in folk-tradition and in different localities. This would account for the variation in details. In this setting the lying and dissimulation of Abram or Isaac would call for no comment, but the sanctity of the marriage bond should be noted. Not even a king will take a woman into his harem while her husband is alive. 2. The story as preserved furnished the material for the 'teachers' of Israel, precisely because it was a popular story. With fine artistry he makes the point that God is able to protect his people when they are helpless, even

when the danger to which they are exposed is the product
of their own lack of trust and moral failure.

## 11. a fair woman
The literary context would make Sarai between 65 and
70 years of age (cf. 17.17; 12.4), and obviously unlikely to
arouse the kind of interest suggested in this story. But no
such figures appear in the story; they derive from the later
(P) additions.

## 13. my sister
She was in fact his half-sister. At a later date marriages
of this kind were forbidden (Lev. 18.11; 20.17), though still
possible during the early monarchy (II Sam. 13.13).

## my soul
In Hebrew usage this is an emphatic way of expressing
the personal pronoun 'I'.

## 15. Pharaoh
The Egyptian word is literally 'The great house' and is
a title of the Eygptian king.

## 16. entreated
i.e. treated. CAMELS. Since these animals were not domesticated until a later period, this is an indication (like the
Philistines in 26.1) of the way in which an ancient story
acquired features appropriate to a later age.

## 17. plagued . . . with great plagues
This seems to the modern reader quite unjust. But that
is not the point of the story. They are indeed evidence of
divine displeasure at the point at which a grave evil is
about to be perpetrated, viz, the taking of a married woman
into the harem. That is how they would be interpreted by
the Pharaoh, and so lead him to seek the cause of the

divine displeasure. They are not penal, but a 'sign' to Pharaoh which lead him to discover the truth.

**18-20.** The sharp rebuke to Abram and the generosity of the Pharaoh may well reflect the 'teacher's' deeper reflection upon Abram's conduct.

## THE SEPARATION OF ABRAM AND LOT

### Ch. 13

The main point of this story is to account for the separation of Lot the ancestor of the Moabites and Ammonites from the Israelite patriarch. Lot also had left Haran, and, since Abram was childless, might well be regarded as heir to the blessing. But, as the conclusion of the story shows, the blessing must go to the true heir, the one whom God has chosen. Lot, in separating from Abram, is cut off from the creative blessing, and the remainder of his story shows his progressive weakness.

The immediate cause of the separation was the great increase in wealth in terms of flocks and herds—a sign of the blessing. The watering places at which they stopped could not support so many. Strife broke out among the herdmen. Abram, as head of the family, took the initiative (v. 8) and with fine oriental courtesy offers the choice to Lot (v. 9). He chose the Jordan-Dead Sea Valley (v. 10) which was well-watered and fertile. There is some evidence that this district which, during the Biblical period as now, was desolate and infertile, was at one time able to support a considerable population. The date of this can hardly be that of the patriarchal period, but Genesis has preserved both the memory of this earlier fertility and of some great catastrophe (ch. 19). It is not suggested that Lot chose this

district knowing of its wickedness; but it may be suggested
that he took advantage of the choice so generously offered
to get the best for himself. Yet the promise requiring faith
is renewed to Abram (vv. 14-17) when he no longer has
a kinsman to whom he may transmit it. It is to be noted
also that Abram still recognizes the sacred obligation of
coming to the help of the stricken kinsman (ch. 14, and the
point is explicitly made by the Priestly teacher in 19.29).

## 18. in the plain of Mamre

Better ' by the oaks or terebinths of Mamre '. MAMRE,
the modern Ramet el Khalil, ' the hill of the friend ' (sc.
of God), is either identical with or in the district of Hebron,
and appears to have been an ancient sacred place.

It should be noted that the beginning and the end of the
story shows the patriarch at the sanctuary altar. Worship
is the interest of the early (J), no less than of the later (P)
teacher.

## ABRAM'S VICTORY OVER THE FOUR KINGS
## AND MEETING WITH MELCHIZEDEK

## Ch. 14

The significance of this story, as it relates that series of
events in which the victorious working of God's saving
purpose is declared, is clear. It is summarized in the poem
of vv. 19 f. No less clear is the ' right response ' of Abram
to him who gave the victory; he will take no reward from
man, since he acted solely at God's command. Perhaps the
incident described in vv. 18-20, which is incidental to the
main story, is deliberately intended to associate Abram
with the city which God chose (SALEM = Jerusalem), where
subsequently the Davidic monarchy ruled. The intention

of the Biblical writer should be clearly recognized and not obscured by the highly perplexing literary and historical phenomena of this chapter.

The style and language make it clear that its origin is other than that of the main strata of the Pentateuch. That is simply to say that the writer has made use of some tradition other than those normally available to him. It would be reasonable to suppose it derives from Jerusalem itself. The historical details referred to suggest that it is an ancient tradition and often repeated.

The names of the invading kings are such as to make it most improbable that they are the invention of a later age. Yet their activity cannot be related to archaeological discovery so far made. The names are known, or shown to be possible, from ancient records. AMRAPHEL cannot be equated with Hammurabi, King of Babylon, but it is a good Babylonian name and in fact appears as the name of a citizen. Its meaning, ' Hammurabi is my god ', suggests a date during or soon after the great king's reign. CHEDORLAOMER would correspond to Kudar Lagamar (servant of the god Lagamar) and is a good Elamite name. It may be equated with Kudur Naḥḥunte, a seventeenth century BC king. TIDAL would appear to be Tudḥalia, a Hittite king name of which the first ruled in the seventeenth century. His title KING OF NATIONS would be appropriate to a leader of an army composed of various groups. ARIOCH may be identified with Ariyuk, a name that appears in the dynasty of Mari. All that can reasonably be said, in the light of archaeological study, is that Gen. 14 gives us a brief glimpse of the unrest of this period when marauding bands of various origins, forced out of their homeland, were seeking booty (cf. v. 11).

We should not expect to identify the Canaanite kings; but the names of the small city states over which they ruled are entirely consistent both with later Biblical accounts and with extra-Biblical accounts of the land. Until the rise of the Davidic monarchy the land of Canaan was divided into a great number of city states and was usually subject to a foreign overlord.

## 3. The vale of Siddim
This is not mentioned elsewhere, and the reference to the SALT SEA suggests that the account of its submergence remained in popular memory (cf. ch. 19).

## 4. they served
i.e. they were vassal kings.

**5, 6.** These tribal names appear also in Deut. 2.10-12, 20, 21. The English plural ' s ' should be omitted in v. 5 since the ending ' -im ' is the Hebrew plural. The HORITES are now known from extra-Biblical sources, to be the Hurrians, a people who exercised sway over a considerable area of Amorite territory in the sixteenth and fifteenth centuries; some of their laws and customs became a permanent part of Canaanite life (cf. 15.2; 16.2; 25.30-34). Subsequent invasions of Ammonites, Moabites, Edomites and Israelites encountered these peoples as they settled in their respective territories. HAM is not, in Hebrew, the same spelling as the name of Noah's son.

**8-10.** Obviously the place of battle was chosen by the five kings because of their familiarity with a difficult terrain. It contained numerous bitumen (AV SLIME) pits, in which some at least hid to escape capture (cf. v. 17).

## 13. the Hebrew
The first occurrence of this word. It is not a common term in the Old Testament and is normally used by non-Israelites (especially Egyptians) or Israelites distinguishing themselves from Egyptians. The term mainly occurs in the patriarchal period and during the sojourn in Egypt. It appears to be not primarily an ethnic term but a term to

C

define status. The application of this term to Abram would be appropriate to a tradition preserved at Jerusalem in pre-Israelite times.

## 14. Dan

Since the name only replaced the earlier Laish at a considerably later date (cf. Judg. 18.29) its use here shows the influence of a later age.

**15.** There are many examples of a night attack by a few, creating wild confusion and panic in a much larger force; in this instance we have not a well disciplined army, but something like a band of freebooters. LEFT HAND, i.e. the Northern side (so RV and RSV).

## 18. Melchizedek king of Salem

Is referred to only here, in Ps. 110.4 and in Heb. chs. 5-7. The NT reference may seem to the modern ear a strange piece of exegesis and hardly convincing. But it is important to realize that the general argument, though not its application to Jesus, must have been securely based in Jewish circles of that time. Recent OT scholarship has gone far to indicate what this background of thought was. SALEM (cf. Ps. 76.2) is the later Jerusalem. But this name is a deliberate modification of the original Urusalem (so the Amarna tablets) a name which means '(the god) Salem founded (the city)'. Either by the omission of the first element, or by its modification, all such pagan associations were removed. Similarly the king's name, originally meaning '(the god) Zedek is King' (cf. Adoni-zedec, Josh. 10.1 'Zedek is my lord') was reinterpreted as King of righteousness. Jerusalem was an ancient Canaanite city with a well-established religious ritual and tradition. Its king was also its chief priestly figure. When David captured the city, he acquired also the prestige attaching to the king of this city, and many of its traditions persisted; this account in Gen. 14

is one. We recognize that David combined the nomadic Israelite way of life with much that belonged to the older Canaanite culture, though the God of Israel replaced the Canaanite deities. He inherited the traditions attaching to the earlier kings of Jerusalem; ' he was anointed after the order of Melchizedek '. This marks the transition from the charismatic leadership which is appropriate to the nomadic Israelite, to the ordered dynastic kingship which is necessary for a settled people. It is to be noticed that David had two sons bearing the older divine name, Absalom, Solomon, and that Zadok was one of his priests. Further, it was Zadok who supported Solomon and at length defeated his rival Abiathar. It is to be noted that the memory of the predominantly non-Israelite character of Jerusalem was alive in Ezekiel's day (cf. Ezek. 16.3). In the light of Gen. 14.18 ff., the ritual words of Ps. 110 can be clearly understood, and, as the Messiah became an eschatological figure this ancient tradition took on further meaning. The argument of Heb. 5-7 is entirely appropriate in this setting. (For a discussion of Ps. 110, cf. A. Johnson, *Sacral Kingship in Ancient Israel*, p. 120-122.)

### bread and wine

i.e. a royal feast. But to eat and drink with another is to establish communion.

### the most high God

cf. Ps. 78.35, also Pss. 7.17; 47.2; 57.2; 78.56. The significance of this becomes clear when we transliterate the Hebrew, which has no article. Melchizedek was the priest of 'El 'Elyon. Both the nouns are known as the names of deities in the Aramean world. It appears that Elyon was, in Jerusalem, identified with El, the high god. This in turn paves the way for the absorption of the powers of the Canaanite deity by Yahweh of Israel.

**19-20.** The blessing is rhythmical in form, and appears to be a ritual formula. It is quite appropriate that the Canaanite King should ascribe the creation of the world to El Elyon. It is to be noted that in v. 22 Abram identifies El Elyon with Yahweh. Again we detect the work of the shrine teacher. He makes it clear that all the great attributes of the gods worshipped in Canaan were in fact attributes of Yahweh.

**he gave him**

   i.e. Abram gave Melchizedek.

**21.** logically follows on v. 17. But the story as we have it in Genesis, with the distinctive divine name in vv. 19, 20 and 22, suggests that it was already a unity before it was written.

## THE FIRST COVENANT WITH ABRAM

### Ch. 15

This chapter, with the promise renewed in a solemn covenant, is one of the foundation stones of the patriarchal tradition. The divine promise, man's response in faith, the covenant between God and man, form a unity which characterizes Biblical religion. It would appear that this story formed part of the sacred tradition of both the Northern and the Southern shrines. This, rather than any political charter, sets forth the real meaning of Israel's life. It is characteristic of the Old Testament that the profound theological ideas preserved in this chapter are presented in the form of a story.

The promise is given in circumstances which appear to offer no possibility of fulfilment (vv. 2 and 3 apparently deriving from E and J respectively). The response sought, and given, is that of absolute trust (v. 6). This is the essential nature of Biblical religion; all worship and all moral attainment springs from this faith. Without it worship becomes sterile and morality a narrow legalism. It is in this faith relationship that the real life of man consists (Hab. 2.4) and, as the Jewish rabbis taught, the Rule of God becomes manifest in human life (cf. I Macc. 2.52). It is this faith in God which provides the human condition in which the sovereign work of God can be manifested. Thus the phrase COUNTED IT TO HIM FOR RIGHTEOUSNESS (v. 6) must be understood. It had its setting in the law-court, and particularly where the king administers justice. Abraham has acted as a loyal subject of God the King in trusting the promise, and so God brings him into the intimacy of fellowship. This is not a reward for faith; rather is faith the kind of response to God in which God may be known. We may paraphrase this as: 'God dealt with Abram as one who, by trusting his whole life to him, was in the right relationship with him, a loyal subject of the divine King' (cf. Rom. 4.3, 9, 22; Gal. 3.6; James 2.23).

The promise is then renewed in terms of the land, and the relationship given concrete expression in the covenant. The conception of religion as a covenant is characteristic of the Bible. It is not a bargain or a contract; it is the free and gracious act of God, 'binding himself' to the one whom he has chosen. Indeed it is remarkable that in this particular covenant nothing is said about any obligations laid on Abram. The sense of obligation springs from within, the spontaneous response of gratitude.

### 1. word of the Lord . . . in a vision
are terms suggestive of the prophets' experience.

### 2. go
i.e. depart from life (cf. Ps. 39.13).

**the steward**

Render 'the heir of my house is Eliezer of Damascus'.
This refers to a practice described in tablets found at Nuzu,
a city state of Northern Mesopotamia, c. 1500 BC. A childless couple might adopt a son, but the inheritance would go
to a true son if one were born. Abram apparently had
already adopted Eliezer.

**12-16.** May be regarded as a parenthesis describing a
mystic vision (cf. Job 33.15) vouchsafed to Abram as the
culmination of the solemn covenant drew near.

**13. stranger**

Better 'sojourner' i.e. a temporary resident.

**four hundred years**

(cf. v. 16) 'in the fourth generation'. It is clear that these
figures cannot be equated and simply indicate the narrator's
indifference to such (for him) details.

**17. a smoking furnace**

A portable earthenware stove normally used for baking
bread. But this strange appearance of smoke and fire becomes a characteristic of a divine appearing (cf. Ex. 19.18).

**19-21.** The tribes referred to indicate the mixed nature of
the Canaanite population, nomad invaders (v. 19), pockets
of earlier invasions and aboriginal peoples.

## THE BIRTH OF ISHMAEL

### Ch. 16

The swift transition from the magnificent outreaching
of faith in ch. 15 to the attempt to force the hand of God
in this chapter is all too human. But more important is the
portrayal of the over-ruling purpose of God both to redeem

man's failure and to fulfil the divine purpose. Sarai's action in giving her slave to Abram reflects a custom recognized in both Hurrian (Biblical 'Horite') and Babylonian law. Her treatment of Hagar (DEALT HARDLY, v. 6, probably means 'branded with a slave mark') was also permitted. Yet the story clearly indicates disapproval of Abram and Sarai and divine judgment in favour of Hagar. She is to bear Abram's son, and although he is not the promised heir, he is to share in the blessing. But especially important is the portrayal of God as the one who hears the cry of the afflicted (v. 11). This is the great characteristic of Israel's God (cf. Ex. 3.7; Deut. 26.7, etc.).

**5.** lit. 'May the violence done to me'. The complaint of Sarai, and the charge that Abram was at fault are completely unjustified, and her treatment of Hagar (v. 6), though possibly legal, was quite unjust by Israelite standards.

**7.** cf **13.** The Angel and the Lord are apparently identified. This is quite appropriate to ancient thought forms, where the agent in the discharge of his mission is regarded as the extension of the personality of the sender (cf. 31.11, 13).

**Shur**
The wall, i.e. the fortified eastern frontier of Egypt.

**11. Ishmael**
i.e. God hears.

**12. a wild man**
Literally 'a wild ass of a man'. The significance of the term may suggest either the free, independent life of the nomadic people of whom Ishmael is regarded as the ancestor (cf. Job 39.5-8), or possibly according to Arabic usage his princely character. The wild ass is a very different

creature from the domesticated animal. IN THE PRESENCE OF—a normal Hebrew phrase for 'to the east of'.

**13,14.** The name of the well makes it clear that it was associated with a theophany, and suggests that it was associated with a sanctuary. It is mentioned again at 24.62; 25.11 as a place connected with Isaac. But the translation of v. 13 and the meaning of the name given to the well are alike obscure. THOU GOD SEEST ME is not a translation of the Hebrew; it appears that the meaning of the name (and perhaps even the pronunciation) has been forgotten, and that it suggested to later Israelite thought the idea of the living and seeing (with compassion) God. The closing phrase in v. 13 may originally have read 'Have I really seen God and remained alive after seeing him' (so RSV with a slight emendation of the text).

## THE COVENANT WITH ABRAM AND THE INSTITUTION OF CIRCUMCISION

### Ch. 17

This chapter is entirely the work of the Priestly writer. It offers a clear example of the reinterpretation character-istic of this teacher of the tradition narrated in ch. 15. A present-day writer would say that the covenant with Abram was full of meaning for Israel under the monarchy; the ex-perience of the Exile and the faith tested by that experi-ence gave new depths of meaning to the ancient story. The old tradition is not superseded; but it has new significance. Thus we may share the faith of the faithful teachers in the Exile who could dare to believe, with Jeremiah and Ezekiel, that God had still a future for his people, and that they would yet return to take up their life in the land of promise. But it was in the Exile that circumcision took on its full sacramental meaning. In pre-exilic days it was a practice common to Israelites and others (though not Philistines, a non-semitic people). Indeed it was practised among many peoples in the ancient world, as it is today; it is known to have been practised in Egypt in 4000 BC. The tradition that the operation must be performed with stone knives (Ex. 4.25; Josh. 5.3) relates the practice to the Stone Age. The rite always had a religious significance, although normally it was a puberty or marriage rite. By it a man became fully a member of the tribal community. Some traces of its original connection with marriage are retained in the Old Testament. The story of Ex. 4.24-26 clearly reflects this, as do the Hebrew words for bridegroom and father-in-law (wife's father), cf. Gen. 34.13 ff., words which are derived from a verb meaning 'to cut'. Ex. 4.24 ff. suggests that it became a normal Israelite practice through their contact with the Midianites. But in Israelite tradition, the rite was transferred to infancy and became a covenant rite; every male child is claimed as a member of the covenant (not merely tribal) community, the people of God. In Babylon, it was a practice which distinguished the Jews from their captors. It therefore became the distinctive mark of the covenant relationship, the more so in that it was one of the few of their religious institutions that could be practised in the 'unclean' land. Sabbaths and certain food laws acquired a similar importance. This ancient sacramental rite proved itself capable of sustaining the faith of Israel and generating creative energies of hope in the darkest hour of their history. For those who thus received it, new depths of meaning became apparent.

## 1. the Almighty God

It is better to transliterate the Hebrew as *El Shaddai*. El is the high god of the Canaanite pantheon. The meaning of Shaddai is uncertain, but the most probable derivation is from a word meaning 'mountain' (cf. I Kings 20.23).

**5. Abram . . . Abraham**

The latter form of the name cannot be etymologically connected with the Hebrew word for 'multitude'; this would require Abhamon. There is no Hebrew word to correspond to *raham* and the attempt to associate it with the Arabic *ruham*—copiousness, well watered—is very doubtful. It is probable that the form Abraham is a deliberate extension of the original Abram, possibly to avoid the pagan associations of that form (lofty Father—*viz.* of the tribe).

**15. Sarai . . . Sarah**

These may be two forms of the same word *sarah* a princess.

**19. Isaac**

i.e. *Yiṣḥāq* possibly originally *Yiṣḥāq-el* '(the god) *El* laughs,' but reinterpreted by relating it to v. 17 (cf. also 18.12 (J); 21.6 (E)).

**20. I have heard thee**

A similar play on the name Ishmael (cf. 16.11 (J)). But here the name is related to Abraham's prayer in v. 18.

**25.** This appears to reflect the age of circumcision among these nomadic peoples.

ABRAHAM'S INTERCESSION

## Ch. 18

With fine artistry this story presents one of the most serious challenges to Israel's faith. Granted that Israel had departed from their ancient faith and proved unworthy, yet there were those who remained loyal to God. Should they

also suffer with the wicked? Do not the prophecies of judgment such as we find in Amos suggest a failure of God's
justice? It is with this problem that some of the greatest
passages in the OT are concerned (e.g. Job, Isa. 52.13–
53.12). It is part of the miracle of Israel's religion that this
problem was faced at so early a date, that it was set forth
in terms of faith, not of abstract discussion of principles,
and that while no final answer is given, the ' way through '
is clearly indicated. The JUDGE OF ALL THE EARTH is no
abstract principle of righteousness; he is personally in-
terested in persons, and acts accordingly.

The promise of a son to Sarah (vv. 1-15) is the setting for
what follows; by this means the hearer's attention was at
once captured. Then comes (vv. 16-22) the disclosure to
Abraham of the divine purpose for SODOM and GOMORRAH;
the interest is heightened, for any reference to the fate of
these cities quickened the imagination of the Israelite.
What follows (vv. 23-33) however, is totally unexpected.
Everybody knew that these cities were wicked and deserv-
ing of divine displeasure; but were there no righteous men
in them? Here, then, is a brilliant example of an OT parable,
the more effective in that it makes use of well-known and
accepted material. So Israel, faithless and disobedient, may
yet be spared the richly deserved calamity for the sake of
the faithful few.

**2-5.** A fine picture of a nomadic sheikh's hospitality towards strangers. He calls it a LITTLE WATER and a MORSEL
OF BREAD, but he provides in fact a sumptuous feast (vv.
6 ff.), and all with the greatest courtesy. THREE MEASURES
(v. 6) is about eight gallons; A CALF was a princely gift, since
flesh is not a normal part of daily food; BUTTER is the
curdled milk much prized by the nomad.

**12.** A second play on the name Isaac (cf. 17.17).

**16-22.** Abraham, the man in whose life the blessing is potent, who has responded in faith, is thus prepared to be the recipient of the divine purpose. This passage is echoed in Amos 3.7.

**19. I know him**

The use of the verb 'to know' in Hebrew is richer than normal English usage (cf. Gen. 4.1; Amos 3.2). It suggests intimacy of relationship. The following words should be rendered 'in order that he may'. God had chosen Abraham in order that a people might be created to embody the divine purpose for mankind.

**20. cry of Sodom**

i.e. the outcry about Sodom.

**22. stood yet before**

This is one of the traditional postures of prayer.

**23-33.** Abraham's intercession is presented in the form natural to the Orient. Formally it is a bargaining process. But the Jahwist was as aware as the Christian saint that man cannot bargain with God. 'Will not the Judge of all the earth perform true justice?' In fact he finds that his own compassion is more than matched by God's.


### THE DESTRUCTION OF SODOM AND GOMORRAH AND THE RESCUE OF LOT

### 19.1-29

The terrible disaster that fell on these cities in the valley of Siddim left a profound mark on the memory of the inhabitants of Canaan, as the number of references in the OT show. No trace of their existence has remained to view, but doubtless the utter sterility of the Dead Sea and its neighbourhood would help to preserve the memory. Recent investigation has suggested that there were cities in the neighbourhood of the Dead Sea, and lends probability to the location of Sodom and Gomorrah beneath the southern end of the lake. If so, their destruction would seem to have taken place long before the patriarchal period. The description of the disaster would be entirely appropriate to the natural conditions of the area. The district is 1,000 ft. below sea-level, part of a great geological fault that extends into Africa. An earthquake, the emission of inflammable gas and oil, and fire produced either by spontaneous combustion or by ignition from domestic fires clearly fit the Biblical picture. Even the fate that befell Lot's wife could find its partial parallel in the fate of some of the victims in Pompei encased in falling débris. That Israelite tradition associated such an event with Abraham is quite natural and in no way impugns the value of the tradition.

But the narrator (J) of this story is not concerned to preserve archaeological material. He is using the well-known story for his purpose. It was an act of God richly merited by the wickedness of the inhabitants of these cities of which one incident of a particularly scandalous kind is given as an example (vv. 5 ff.). To the teachers of Israel, disasters were not mere happenings; they were interpreted as acts of God, evidence of his moral government of the world. To establish the historicity of an event and its natural causes is a desirable and sometimes necessary discipline. The man of God is concerned to see in the event the hand of God. The event and the interpretation form a unity, the interpretation (if it be inspired by God) being both the product of faith and creative of deeper faith.

**1-9.** Lot, like Abraham, offered generous hospitality, and even defended them against the attacks of the citizens, though the lengths to which he was prepared to go cannot be approved. It is perhaps implied that, by living in Sodom, a weakening of his moral judgment has taken place.

**10 ff.** The iniquity of the inhabitants has been brought to light. Justice must be done, and it must be seen to be done.

### 11. blindness
A word that occurs only here and II Kings 6.18. It probably means the effect of dazzling light.

### 14. mocked
Better ' jested ' (cf. RSV).

### 15. iniquity
As commonly in the OT the iniquity and its consequent punishment are thought of as one, and the same word is used for both (so the margin). It is translated ' punishment ' in I Sam. 28.10.

### 22. Zoar
One of the five cities whose name suggested the verb ' to be little ', a characteristic Hebrew assonance.

### 25. overthrew
Literally ' turned upside down ', which strongly suggests an earthquake.

### 26. a pillar of salt
Either this refers to a rock formation to which later ages attached the name ' Lot's wife ', or it describes her fate as, overcome by the fumes, her body was covered with the fine ash produced by the explosion of natural gas. But this feature of the tradition is made to serve the teacher's interest: SHE LOOKED BACK, cf. Luke 17.32.

**29.** The Priestly writer's comment draws attention to the rescue of Lot as the consequence of God's relationship with Abraham.

## MOAB AND AMMON

### 19.30-38

This story, though repugnant to us, is a typical example of coarse popular humour. It should be noted that these tribal names are not connected etymologically with the Hebrew words for 'father' (*'ab*) and 'people' (*'am*). The word-play indicates Judean hatred of these nations together with a recognition of kinship. In fact, they spoke practically the same language as the Israelites and shared many of their customs. But the 'teacher' has made use of this story, just because it was popular, to make his point; moral corruption invades the life of those who associate themselves with evil.

## ABRAHAM AND ABIMELECH

### 20.1-18

This is the story of 12.10-20 as it was told apparently in the Northern Kingdom. The distinctive features in this account are (i) the partial justification of Abraham's deceit in that Sarah is explicitly described as his half-sister (v. 12); (ii) the revelation to the pagan king in a dream (vv. 3 ff.) with its explicit recognition of that king's integrity (v. 6); and (iii) the description of Abraham as a prophet with the role of intercessor (v. 7). The over-all purpose in narrating this story is to emphasize the sovereign protection given to Abraham and Sarah to whom the divine blessing has been given, and through whom the divine purpose is to be fulfilled, although in this story they are 'of little faith'.

## 1. Gerar
If this is the same as in 10.19 and 26.1 it is near Gaza in the territory that became Philistine, though this does not well suit the clause DWELLED BETWEEN KADESH AND SHUR. SOJOURNED IN GERAR is, in Hebrew, a word-play, '*wayyagor bigerar*'.

## 3. thou art but a dead man
He was rendered impotent.

## 4. righteous
i.e. in the right with regard to this matter.

**6.** The marriage bond is a sacred relationship, under divine sanction.

**7.** The description of Abraham as a prophet draws attention to the fact that prophets were more than 'spokesmen of God'. They were recipients of the divine commands for and on behalf of the people of God. They were recipients also of divine energy to bring the divine will to fulfilment. It is as the man of the blessing that his soul is filled with mysterious power and thus he intercedes for Abimelech, cf. v. 17. (In Ps. 105.15 all the patriarchs are described as prophets.)

## all that are thine
The life of the people was understood to be so bound up with the life of the king that his conduct immediately affected them (cf. II Sam. 24.10 ff.).

**9-11.** With fine irony the point is made that the pagan displays greater reverence (fear of God) and a higher standard of moral obligation than does the patriarch.

### 13. thy kindness

The Hebrew word means that devoted loyalty that is appropriate to the marriage-bond.

**14 ff.** Abimelech made princely 'compensation' for the wrong he had inadvertently done to Abraham, and for the no less inadvertent shame he had brought upon Sarah. The weight of the silver would be about 26 lbs.

## THE BIRTH OF ISAAC

### 21.1-7

The Priestly teacher has made use of ancient traditions in order to emphasize the importance of circumcision.

The ages of Abraham and Sarah are not meant to be taken literally, and no attempt to relate these figures to other incidents can be successful. In the following story Ishmael would be sixteen years old according to 16.16 and not the infant of 21.14-16. The difficulties for us are caused by confusing the ancient story with the Priestly teacher's comments. It is possible that he intended to relate the age of Abraham at the birth of Isaac to that of Shem at the birth of his first-born after the Flood. The birth of Isaac is thus a new beginning in the salvation history of man. The ages of the patriarchs are clearly intended to have some such symbolic value.

**6.** The name Isaac is again connected with laughter, but this time the laughter of joy. In v. 9 it is connected with 'playing' (AV, MOCKING). All these words are from the same Hebrew verb.

D

## THE EXPULSION OF HAGAR AND ISHMAEL

### 21.8-21

Ishmael, though not the child of promise, is yet the son of Abraham and partakes of his father's soul and blessing. In popular tradition the Ishmaelites were a kindred people to the Israelites, but also hostile (cf. Ps. 83.6). But the narrator would suggest that they too were under the care of the God of Israel.

**8. was weaned**
This was normally at two years old or older (cf. II Macc. 7.27) in the East and was the occasion of a family feast.

**10 ff.** Abraham's conduct was both inhuman and illegal. God acts to right the wrong done to Hagar and her child.

**14. a bottle**
The skin of an animal prepared for carrying water. We should probably render '. . . and he placed the child on her shoulder' (cf. RSV).

**15.** Render at the end of the verse 'and the child lifted up his voice and wept' and connect with v. 16.

**17-19.** The divine messenger and God are virtually identified (cf. 16.7, 13).

**21. Paran**
The district south of Judah and west of Edom.

## ABRAHAM AND ABIMELECH

### 21.22-34

It appears that this story was originally a continuation of
20.1-17, although some details preserved in the Southern
tradition have been included in the final form (vv. 25 f.,
28 f.). Evidence of the influence of later experience may be
seen in the reference to Philistines in vv. 32, 34, who did
not settle in the land until the twelfth century, some five
hundred years after Abraham's time.

Originally the story was told as a means of establishing
in folk memory the ancient Israelite right to use the oasis at
Beer-sheba. This right of access to water and pasture is
one of fundamental importance in the life of the nomad,
and the traditions establishing the right were faithfully and
carefully preserved; it was essential that they should be.
The scarcity of water and pasture in this part of the world
demands that only certain tribes may use a given well. Par-
ticipating tribes entered into a solemn covenant, each
guaranteeing the rights of the other, and the gods of the
contracting partners would be involved, providing a religious sanction to the covenant.

It is possible to recognize that this story was preserved
in two traditions (and apparently a third form appears in
26.15-33), the one in vv. 22-24, 27, 31 (E); the other in vv.
25-26, 28-30, 33 (J). In the former the name BEER-SHEBAH
is connected with the Hebrew word 'to swear on oath'
(shāba‘), in the latter with the Hebrew word for 'seven'
(sheba‘).

The shrine priest has taken this ancient tradition and
emphasized the divine protection of the father of his people,
a protection that is manifest to the pagan. Abraham is the
living evidence of the divine blessing. It is evident from vv.
32 and 34 that the story was thus told after the Israelites

had settled in Canaan and after the days when the Philistine territory was clearly defined, i.e. during the monarchy period.

## 22. Phichol
The linguistic origin of this name, other than the fact that, unlike Abimelech, it is non-Semitic, cannot be certainly determined. It may be derived from the Egyptian word for Lydian, or be a corrupted form of a genuinely Philistine name.

## God is with thee . . .
The recognition of the power of the blessing; therefore it is of great advantage to enter into a covenant with Abraham.

## 23. that thou wilt not
The margin 'if thou wilt' simply reproduces the closing phrase of the oath-form: 'God do so to thee and more also if thou wilt . . .' The opening phrase was frequently omitted.

## my son . . . my son's son
An alliterative phrase in Hebrew which might be rendered 'my kith and kin' (cf. Isa. 14.22; Job 18.19). KINDNESS is a quite inadequate translation. Abimelech is saying 'I have loyally performed every obligation towards you, a sojourner, and you must reciprocate'.

## 25. reproved
The word is a legal term: 'charged him' as in a court of law.

## 27.
The giving and receiving of a gift is a means of establishing fellowship, and this is given concrete expression in the covenant making.

## 33. grove
Render 'tamarisk tree'. (So I Sam. 22.6; 31.13.)

## THE SUPREME TEST OF FAITH

### 22.1-19

The dignity and restrained emotion of this literary masterpiece are apparent. But the literary qualities are the product of a deep religious insight. There could be no finer presentation of faith and obedience, not counting the cost, until we see Jesus on the Cross. It is to be noted that the Epistle to the Hebrews cites this story in its roll-call of faith (Heb. 11.17-19). In terms of man's response to God, this is what religion means.

It would appear that the shrine teacher has made use of a well-known story connected with an ancient cult centre whose name is obscured in v. 14. The story may also have been used at one time to justify the repudiation in the Israelite tradition of the Canaanite practice of human sacrifice. But it should be noted that the story as it is told in Genesis does not make this point. In view of the explicit prohibition in the Law this would not be necessary. The sacrifice of Isaac is required and averted by God, and Abraham's willingness is praised by God. The story is told, not merely as an incident in the life of Abraham, nor as an example to be literally followed, but, in parabolic fashion, as a challenge to faith. God's dominion is absolute; man's response in faith and obedience must be unreserved.

The point of this story becomes clear when we recall (as the Israelite would) the setting of the story in Genesis. The beginning of the Abraham story records how he ' left all ' in obedience to the divine summons (12.1). He received the blessing and the promise which could in fact only be fulfilled through a son, the fruit of his marriage to Sarah. This is the meaning of Abraham's life, his faith and experience. The test of his loyal obedience was quite literally a ' self-noughting ' (cf. Mark 8.35). With the death of Isaac, all

Abraham's hopes were doomed. But the reader of the story also knows that Isaac was saved to become the transmitter of the blessing. His interest is at once kindled; he wants to know how this 'impossible' situation can be resolved. Clearly no solution is possible at the human level. Only God, who tested Abraham in such a way as to demonstrate the fullness of faith and obedience, can 'provide' the means whereby the divine purpose can be fulfilled. The reader knows this, but in the nature of the case, Abraham could not until God 'provided'; he must obey and trust. This was the lesson that Israel had to learn in the long discipline of history. It was never more to the point than in the tragedy of total invasion and exile. There is some evidence in the story that the wise teachers of Israel related this story both to the tragedy of the Northern Kingdom (vv. 1-13, 19 (E)) and to Judah (13-18 (J)). At an early date the Christian Church in its liturgy related this story to the Passion of Christ. It seems that St Paul had this passage in mind in his presentation of the love of God (Rom. 8.32). In the Epistle to the Hebrews (11.17-19) this offering of his only son is the final proof of Abraham's faith.

**1.** In the Hebrew sentence GOD is emphatic. 'It was God who tested . . .'

**2.** The pathos is finely expressed in the series of accusatives '. . . THY SON, THINE ONLY SON WHOM THOU LOVEST, ISAAC . . .'

The location of MORIAH cannot be determined and was evidently unknown at an early date. Some Jewish traditions associate it with Jerusalem (cf. II Chron. 3.1), but this is improbable; Jerusalem was at this time a Jebusite city.

**4-8.** The head of the family was the normal officiant at a sacrifice in the earlier period. GOD WILL PROVIDE—the phrase is taken up in v. 14 (q.v.), literally 'God will see for himself'.

**12.** The proof of Abraham's faith is expressed in the phrase 'I know that you fear God'. This is not a servile cringing fear, but reverence which can include, or be included in, love (Deut. 10.12) and issues in obedience. But in Hebrew there is a play on words 'One who fears God' (*yerē*); LOOKED, v. 13 (*yar'*); PROVIDE v. 8 (*yir'eh*); IT SHALL BE SEEN, v. 14 (*yērā'eh*); are all associated with the place name given as JEHOVAH-JIREH (*Yahweh-yir'eh*). This is a common device in the telling (and remembering) of a story by which the mind is prepared for the climax.

**13.** In the modern sense of the word there is no suggestion of miracle in the RAM CAUGHT IN A THICKET. But in the Biblical sense it was a miracle. That is, it was an event (which might or might not be 'ordinary') in which the perceptive man saw God at work. For example, the plagues of Egypt were not miracles to the Egyptians, but for Moses they were signs of God's work for saving his people (cf. Num. 14.22).

The name JEHOVAH-JIREH is a most improbable place-name, and has apparently replaced a name like Jeruel (II Chron. 20.6). The location of Jeruel near Tekoa would suit the story. If this is correct, the story originally had to do with a manifestation of God which caused the place to become a cult-centre (cf. 28.11-22, especially v. 19). But the narrator has ignored that particular interest in order the more effectively to make his point. This is clear in the Hebrew of the place-name and the closing words 'Jehovah (Yahweh) sees', 'the Lord (Yahweh) is seen' or 'appears'.

**15-19.** Here the teacher of Israel draws out the further implications of the story. The blessing is renewed. This is not mere repetition. Rather is it that Abraham, by his unqualified faith and complete obedience, is able to receive the blessing in all its fullness.

**16. saith the Lord**

Corresponds to a Hebrew word which appears in the
Pentateuch only again at Num. 14.28, but frequently in the
Prophets; literally 'Oracle of Yahweh'. What Abraham has
done has consequence for all generations of Israel.

## AN ARAMAEAN TRIBAL GROUP

### 22.20-24

This brief note prepares the mind of the reader for the
narrative in Ch. 24. It is not what we would understand by
a genealogy but a normal Old Testament way of describing
a tribal confederation (cf. 25.13-16). The names refer to
tribes, who lived east of the Jordan. Some of these tribes
are referred to in other parts of the Old Testament (cf. Job
1.1; 32.2; Jer. 25.20, 23, etc.), while others are known from
Mesopotamian documents. During the monarchy period,
the fortunes of Israel were closely bound up with those of
ARAM (Syria).

## THE DEATH AND BURIAL OF SARAH (P)

### Ch. 23

One interesting feature of this story is that the transaction
accords with what is now known of Hittite law as it appears
in an ancient Hittite Code found at Boghazköy in Turkey.
Clearly the Hittites in the Genesis story, although long
before this separated from the peoples of Asia Minor, had
retained many of their ancestral customs. The Hittite Code
belongs to the fourteenth century BC, but reflects well-
established customs from a much earlier period. In that law,

the possession of a property carries with it certain obligations towards the overlord.[1] The transfer of that property carried the feudal obligation with it, unless only a part of it was transferred. This explains Abraham's original wish to have only the cave, and the owner's insistence that he must buy the whole property. The specific mention of the trees in v. 17 is also in accordance with Hittite custom. The politeness and courtesy that mark the negotiation are characteristic of an Oriental transaction. In fact it is a piece of hard bargaining, in spite of the fact that no 'gentleman' would ever talk of selling! Even the monetary value is mentioned only incidentally (v. 15).

It should be noted also that this chapter belongs to the latest stratum in the Pentateuch and was incorporated into the Genesis tradition in the post-exile era. Since Hittite laws and customs were obviously unknown at that time, it is a useful reminder of the faithfulness with which ancient traditions were preserved. This is however only surprising to the Western mind which, especially since the invention of printing, is dependent on the printed word. In many parts of the world it is normal to preserve traditions of the remote past by oral transmission.

But, why was this story recorded? There is no evidence in the Old Testament that Sarah, still less her tomb, was an object of special veneration. Indeed, ancient Israel was remarkably free from ancestor worship, or cults of the dead. It is true that Abraham, Isaac and Rebekah, Jacob and Leah were also buried there. Yet no special sanctity appears to have attached to the tomb so far as is known. The point seems to be that Abraham must die, as he lived, in faith, possessing, of the land promised to him, only a burial place and a well (21.22-34). The acquisition of this property is an 'earnest of his inheritance', a mark of his faith in the future fulfilment of the divine promise (cf. Heb. 11.13).

[1] Cf. J. B. Pritchard, *Ancient Near Eastern Texts*, O.U.P., 1950, p. 191.

## 2. Kirjath-arba

'The city of four (quarters)', is frequently referred to as the original name for Hebron (cf. 35.27; Josh. 14.15, etc.). The mourning and weeping refer not only to Abraham's personal grief but also to the rites and lamentations prescribed for the occasion. (The Book of Lamentations is composed of carefully constructed mournings for the 'dead' city.) The Hebrew word here for MOURN means 'to beat the breast'.

## 3. sons of Heth

i.e. the Hittites—an expression peculiar to the Priestly tradition.[1]

## 4. stranger and sojourner

Better 'sojourner and settler', indicating Abraham's status as one who had limited rights in the land, but was not a full member of the community.

## give

A polite way of saying 'sell' which everyone understood. The courteous language continues throughout the conversation.

## 6. mighty prince

is literally 'a prince of God'. Such a phrase, while it might well be, on the lips of the speakers, no more than a courteous greeting as in our versions, would have overtones for the Priestly writer.

## 8. communed

The Hebrew word is the regular verb for 'spoke' (so also 18.33; 34.6, 8, 20; 42.14; 43.19).

[1] For a good introduction to Hittite history and culture, cf. O. R. Gurney, *The Hittites*, Pelican, London, 1952.

**9. Machpelah**

appears to mean 'the double place' and to refer to the district rather than the cave only (cf. v. 17). The cave is believed to be under the mosque of Hebron, and was venerated in pre-Islamic days by Jews and Christians.

**10. all that went in at the gate**

i.e. the citizens, who have the right to decide on communal matters.

**13-18.** It is characteristic of this tradition to give precise details of the legal transaction. The value can hardly be estimated, except to say that the weight of the silver was about 9 lbs.

## THE MARRIAGE OF ISAAC

## Ch. 24

The narrative in this chapter is a fine example of the story-teller's art. It abounds in those vivid details, repetitions, and incidental comments that mark it as a narrative told and told again long before it was written down. It is a story that people never tired of hearing. That is what made it valuable material for the wise teacher of his people concerning God's providential care and guidance even in so domestic an affair as a marriage. The external scenes are hardly important; the action takes place in the mind of faithful and obedient people.

The story (the longest in the book of Genesis relating a single event) is strikingly different from the stories about Abraham and Jacob, and somewhat resembles in its mode the stories of Joseph in Egypt. It is in the best sense of the word a romance, and, except for the fact that it is so thoroughly Oriental, time and place are insignificant. The truth of the story lies in the fact that God guides even when men are quite unaware of his guidance.

Two thoughts dominate the movement of the story. The one is that Isaac's wife is chosen by God. What appears to be the very large element of chance in the meeting with Rebekah is for the teller evidence of God's action. The other thought is that Isaac must not leave the land of promise. It is still only the land of promise, yet it is where Isaac belongs. Thus the story is dominated by the thought of the divine promise which is to be transmitted from Abraham to Isaac and so to his descendants, and the story, for all its ' popular ' nature, is subordinated to this theme; cf. vv. 1-9, 12, 27, 50, 56, 67. Thus it appears as a fine example of the use made by a faithful teacher of a well-known story to confirm and strengthen the lives of the people of God. The location (v. 62) suggests that this teaching was given in Judaean quarters, perhaps at the shrine of Kadesh which is in the vicinity of BEER-LAHAI-ROI (cf. 16.14). But there is little to indicate the date at which such teaching was given. What can be said is that the popular story, so adapted, proved its worth in the life of the people of God. The promises of God to the patriarchs are sure, whatever may be the circumstances of the historical situation.

**1-9.** *The Oath.* Isaac must not marry a Canaanite woman but one from his father's tribe. At one level, this is a normal custom in the ancient world; at a deeper level it is interpreted as a necessity to maintain the integrity of those who have known the ' call of God '.

**1.** Abraham's great age and prosperity are traditionally interpreted as the direct result of divine blessing; WELL STRICKEN IN YEARS, i.e. he was a very aged man.

**2.** There is no evidence that the SERVANT was ELIEZER (15.2), and since the story was originally independent of the earlier narrative, the inference that he was so is without justification. Throughout this story he remains nameless. SERVANT (literally 'slave') means more than we usually associate with the word. He is part of the family of the head of the house; he may inherit (15.2 f.), and be entrusted with a highly confidential mission, as here, and be treated with great courtesy and respect. On a mission of this kind, he is the fully accredited representative of his lord. (This is what gives especial point to the role of the Servant in Isaiah 53.)

**Put . . . thy hand under my thigh**

(cf. 47.29.) The THIGH is a euphemism for the genital organ (cf. 46.26; Ex. 1.5; Judg. 8.30 where the same Hebrew word is translated 'loins', 'body'). This seems to have been an ancient mode of solemn oath-taking, no longer in use among the later Israelites. A similar practice is reported from other parts of the world. The usual Israelite oath was ' as Yahweh (God) lives' (Judg. 8.19, etc.).

**3. the Lord, the God of heaven**

is a mark of later belief, a natural addition to the original tradition as the story was told in the light of a deepened faith. The phrase occurs in fact only in later literature (cf. Jonah 1.9; Ezra 1.2) and would suggest that it was added when the story was written down.

**7.** A distinctive feature of the narrative is the emphasis on faith. This is especially appropriate, since these are the last recorded words of Abraham. Indeed the scene strangely suggests a death-bed commission (cf. 47.29); this is supported by v. 36 where Isaac has received his father's property; and v. 65 where Isaac replaces Abraham as the servant's master. What follows in 25.1-11 refers to events preceding those of ch. 24.

**his angel**

is hardly an independent figure and suggests simply that God would guide the servant.

**10-27.** *The Meeting with Rebekah.* The reader is swiftly transferred to the district of the Upper Euphrates where Nahor had settled. The latter name appears in texts of the city state of Mari (eighteenth century BC) as the name of a town near Haran. Then follows the all-important meeting with Isaac's destined wife (cf. vv. 14, 44).

**10. camels**

Would appear to be an anachronism, since the evidence indicates that they were not domesticated at the time of the narrative. Probably asses appeared in the original form.

**all the goods**

The AV is ambiguous. What is meant is that the servant was carrying many valuables from his master (cf. RSV).

**11.** Evening and morning were the normal times for the women of the household to draw water; inevitably, as they waited their turn, it was an occasion for giving and receiving information.

**12.** The prayer for success (literally 'cause to happen before me' as in 27.20) leads to the motif of the story in vv. 21, 40, 42, 56, a journey that will be successful.

**shew kindness**

(cf. vv. 14, 27). The AV translation is inadequate. The verb means 'to do'; the noun defies consistent translation by one word. It is a concrete rather than an abstract noun, and indicates an action appropriate to one member of the covenant relationship on behalf of another. We might render: 'fulfil his covenant of love'.

**14.** The test is that of natural human kindness which is, however, more than can reasonably be expected, since it also involved drawing water for the stranger's beast of burden, a considerable labour! The water had to be drawn from the spring to fill the trough. This is a fine anticipation of our Lord's saying in Matt. 5.41.

**15 f.** That these qualities should be shown by the daughter of Abraham's relative, unmarried and beautiful, is an answer to prayer going beyond expectation. It is not easy to determine from Genesis Rebekah's precise relationship to Abraham (cf. vv. 15, 24, 47, 48; cf. also 29.5 where her brother Laban is described as Nahor's son). It is probable that the genealogy has been abbreviated.

**22.** The gift reflects not so much the worth of the service given as that of the giver whom the servant represents.

**27. truth**
in modern English is too abstract; render 'faithfulness'.

**28-60.** The meeting with Laban.

**29 f.** The text would read more smoothly if 29b followed 30a after UNTO ME. In 30b the Hebrew should be rendered 'the man *was standing*' (cf. RSV). It is possible that in v. 30 there is a subtle hint at Laban's avarice of which the Jacob story speaks in greater detail.

**37-48** is mainly a recapitulation more characteristic of a story told than of a story written.

**49. kindly and truly**
These are the same words as in v. 27 and cf. v. 12. It is an appeal for faithful discharge of family obligation.

**50.** Laban's recognition of Yahweh's blessing is a decisive moment in the story. He can do nothing but accept, for the evidence so skilfully presented by the servant demonstrates the activities and purpose of Yahweh.

### 53. precious things
Or ' choice gifts ' represent the price paid to the family by the bridegroom for the bride (cf. 34.12 and Ex. 22.16 RSV; AV and RV mistakenly suggest a dowry). Rebekah's consent is taken for granted; marriages were normally arranged by the parents. The note in v. 67, where love follows marriage, is in complete accord with this.

**54.** So hasty a departure would be quite contrary to normal procedure; perhaps it is to be explained by the fact that Abraham's days were obviously few. The servant who had received the command of the enfeebled Abraham would wish to delay no longer in hope of discharging his commission to his master. Understandably, the family is unwilling, but Rebekah consents. Perhaps the suggestion is intended that she, already in intention and by law part of Abraham's family, has become sensitive to the God of Abraham. We should note however that a law quoted in the Nuzi tablets suggests that the girl's consent was necessary when her brother instead of her father gave her in marriage; and the father is strikingly absent from v. 55, and his name in v. 50, following that of his son, can hardly be original (cf. also v. 59). In v. 60, the blessing is a conventional Oriental one, rhythmic in form, literally

O our sister, become thou    thousands of ten thousand
And may thy seed possess    the gate of their foes

So, with great artistic skill, the Aramaeans are represented as unwittingly echoing the blessing given to Abraham in 22.17.

**61-67.** *Rebekah and Isaac*. The main facts are clear but the details are obscure.

## 62. came from the way of

Is hardly a translation, and the Hebrew can hardly give a meaning.

The ancient versions would suggest a slight emendation to read 'came through' the wilderness to BEER (the well of) —LAHAI-ROI (cf. 16.13 f.), or 'had come from Beer-lahai-roi' (RSV). It is probable that the story originally contained a reference to Abraham's death which was omitted in view of 25.8 ff.

## 63. meditate

Is an improbable guess based on the Greek and Latin versions of the meaning of a verb which occurs only here. A similar Arabic word would suggest the meaning 'to roam' so, 'went out for a walk' (thus the Syriac version).

**67.** Presents grammatical difficulties. We should omit HIS MOTHER SARAH'S (so RSV) and at the end of the verse read 'was comforted after his *father's* death'. Again the addition to the *written* story of ch. 25.7-11 has caused this modification of this last phrase.


## ABRAHAM'S DEATH AND BURIAL

### 25.1-18

(1-6, 11b, 18 (J); 7-11a, 12-17 (P)). A Summary of Tribal Relationships (cf. I Chron. 1.32-33; 29.31).

To the Western reader these lists of names appear irrelevant and pointless. For the nomad and for those living in close contact with nomadic people, they were of great

E

importance. A properly educated man knew these 'genealogies' by heart. There were times when it was a matter of life or death to be able to establish such relationships. The first list (1-4) may well derive from a Judaean source of the semi-nomadic period. The second list (12-16) is of a somewhat different character and describes a twelve-tribe confederacy resembling that of Israel. Most of the names in these lists are known from Biblical and extra-Biblical sources to be the names of districts and tribal groups in South-west Palestine and North-west Arabia. Presented in this way, this section is saying: 'In externals and in terms of ethnic relationships there is no significant difference between Israel and other Eastern Mediterranean peoples. The difference lies in the divine choices and blessing, transmitted through Isaac, son of Abraham.'

## 1. Keturah
Referred to in I Chron. 1.32 as a concubine in order to emphasize the difference between the chosen people and the rest. Only in Israel was the true worship of God maintained.

## 2. Midian
The tribes among whom Moses found refuge, who apparently worshipped Yahweh (cf. Ex. 18); they also invaded Canaan in the Judges period (Judg. 6-8). SHUAH (cf. Job 2.11).

## 3. Sheba and Dedan
(cf. 10.7) a different tradition preserved of SHEBA (i.e. the Sabaeans) who were a well-known mercantile people in Old Testament times (cf. I Kings 10; Jer. 6.20; Ezek. 27.22 ff.).

## Asshurim
Not the Assyrians but an Arabian tribe (cf. v. 18).

**4. Ephah**
cf. Isa. 60.6.

**5.** as in 24.36.

**6.** The children of the slave-wives are given their freedom, but Isaac alone is the true heir.

**7-11.** *Death and burial of Abraham* (P). That this note is from Priestly sources, as its formal style indicates, should not obscure the fact that the material in it is based on carefully preserved tradition. It is closely associated with 23.17-20.

**7.** Abraham, the man of the blessing, lived to a ripe old age (cf. 35.29; Job 42.17). It is characteristic of the Old Testament to present death in such circumstances, as an event to be positively accepted when life has been fulfilled; it is not an event to be feared.

**8. gave up the ghost**
In Hebrew one word, ' expired ', normally a poetic synonym for ' died '. WAS GATHERED TO HIS (father's) PEOPLE is formally incorrect, since the term is properly applicable to the family grave. But by the time of the Priestly work the phrase had lost its literal meaning and meant simply ' was buried ' (cf. v. 17).

**9. Ishmael**
In the light of his permanent separation from Abraham's territory in ch. 21, we must conclude that P was unfamiliar with the early tradition preserved in that chapter.

**12-18.** The Twelve-tribe Confederacy of Ishmael (cf. 17.20).

**12.** These are the generations—apparently the title of an ancient record preserved in Priestly circles and it may well be that it formed the original nucleus of the subsequent Priestly tradition. The term appears eleven times in Genesis and at Num. 3.1.

### 13. Nebajoth and Kedar

cf. Isa. 60.7. MIBSAM and MISHMA (v. 14) appear in I Chron. 4.25 as Simeonite clans. Elements of former nomadic tribes were included with this Israelite tribe, which subsequently lost its identity (cf. 49.7). MASSA: cf. Prov. 30.1; 31.1 where the word ' prophecy ' (AV) ' oracle ' (RV) incorrectly translates MASSA, the name of a tribe (cf. RSV).

### 15. Hadar

Or Hadad (the ' r ' and ' d ' are very similar letters in the Hebrew manuscripts), commonly the name of the supreme god of the Aramaeans, but also an Edomite name (36.35). TEMA (cf. Isa. 21.13 f.; Jer. 25.23; Job 6.19). JETUR, NAPHISH (cf. I Chron. 5.19). JETUR appears to be the Ituraeans of Luke 3.1.

### 16. towns . . . castles

Better ' villages . . . encampments ', although even the former may have been temporary settlements. These tribes would be nomadic or semi-nomadic within the territory of North-west Arabia (v. 18).

So ends the account of Abraham the father of the faithful. He is presented as the man of faith, yet with no attempt to idealize him. He has ' many of the imperfections to which we are all heir, with an uncommon share of the perfections we would like to have '[1] In his failures and in his victories we are made to see one unfailing purpose at work, reaching towards fulfilment, the purpose of God.

[1] B. Vawter, *A Path Through Genesis*, Sheed and Ward, London, 1955, p. 184.

# B. JACOB 25.19–36.43

## THE BIRTH AND YOUTH OF ESAU AND JACOB

### 25.19-34

From this point until 36.43, the main interest is in Jacob, from whom the Israelites traced their descent. Formally this section is described as the history of Isaac and his descendants, but most of the material concerns Jacob/ Israel. What is told in narrative about Isaac (ch. 26) is little more than a duplicate of an incident in the life of Abraham (chs. 12 and 20). Isaac is in fact little more than the one who transmits the blessing from Abraham to Jacob.

The section begins with a characteristic chronological and genealogical note from P (vv. 19 f.) and then draws its material from the Southern tradition (J).

**20. Padan-aram**

P's alternative name for Aram-Naharaim (J).

The stories that follow give clear indications of their original place in the life of Israel. There are word-plays and popular explanations of Israel's superiority over Edom (usually a vassal state of Judah during the monarchy) such as are entirely appropriate to folk-lore. But in making these popular stories the preface to the main account of Jacob the reader is compelled to see them in a new light. Jacob's ' grasping ' nature nearly cost him his life, certainly brought about his flight from home and family and the loss of any hope of effectively gaining his inheritance. Yet it was still the divine purpose that the blessing should be his; Israel is the people of God's choice. Jacob must learn by his self-

defeat to receive what he cannot grasp. The only hint of
this to appear in these two stories is in the oracle (v. 23)
and perhaps the brief phrase at the end of v. 34.

First, particular attention is drawn to the divine activity.
God caused the barren Rebekah to conceive and give birth
to twins. In ancient Israel, every birth was evidence of
God's activity (cf. Ps. 139.13-16 and the rabbinical saying
that father, mother and God ' are, so to speak, partners in
bringing the child to life '). But the point is emphatically
made in v. 21. TO ENQUIRE OF THE LORD (v. 22) would have
the meaning in ancient Israel of consulting the oracle at
the shrine (? Beer-sheba), where the answer would be given
by a cult prophet (cf. I Sam. 9.9; I Kings 22.5; II Kings 1.2),
or a priest (cf. Judg. 18.5 f.). The answer is given in rhythmical form : —

> Two nations in thy body
> Two peoples from thy womb shall be separated
> One people shall become stronger than the other
> The elder shall serve the younger

The point would be obvious to the Israelite; Edom was in
fact a settled kingdom long before the Israelites came into
Canaan, and were subjugated under David. The former
fact is noted in 36.31 (cf. Num. 24.18).

## 25. Red
(*'admoni*) brings to mind Edom; HAIRY (*sē'ār*) calls to mind
Seir (*sē'ir*); Esau would also suggest a word meaning
' hairy ' which does not appear in the Old Testament but
is known from Arabic.

## 26.
Jacob does not mean ' seize by the heel ' but, probably,
' (God) will protect '. Yet the form of the name in Hebrew
*ya'aqob* would suggest ' heel ' (*'aqeb*) or, as in 27.36, ' catch
by the heel ', a metaphor for supplant or over-reach. Jer.

9.4 makes skilful use of this assonance, and we might render the phrase 'every brother plays the Jacob'. It is remarkable that in both the instances of twins referred to in the Old Testament, here and 38.27-30, the younger gains superiority. It is of course a not infrequent theme in folklore.

**27.** Esau became a nomad, living by his skill as a hunter, while Jacob became a shepherd, one who lived on good terms with his fellows, accepting the obligations of an ordered clan-life (AV PLAIN, RSV 'quiet'). Hostility was inevitable, a hostility that is historically reflected in the OT accounts of the relations between Edom and Israel (cf. Num. 20.14-21; II Sam. 8.14; II Kings 8.22; Amos 1.11-12; Obad. 10-11).

The story that follows is quite realistic. The hunter's life is one of alternating plenty and want; in that respect the shepherd's life is more stable. If the hunter fails to kill the quarry, he must go hungry.

**29.** 'Jacob was boiling a stew' (AV SOD POTTAGE) whose main ingredients were red lentils.

**30.** 'Let me gulp some of the red stuff—that red stuff there, for I am famished', and again the sound of the word for red is linked with EDOM.

**31 ff.** The advantage that Jacob took of his brother must not be judged by later standards. The skill to turn a situation immediately to one's own advantage is, in many societies, regarded as commendable. It should be noted that the transaction, whatever be our estimate of it on ethical grounds, was entirely legal. A similar transaction has appeared in a tablet from Nuzi, a Hurrian (Biblical Horite) town south-east of Nineveh (c. 1500 BC). No doubt, as the story was popularly told, it appealed to the sense of

humour of the hearers as they heard the way in which the
ancestor of Israel 'got the better of' the ancestor of the
Edomites. *Their* moral feelings were affronted by the frivo-
lous attitude of Esau to the birthright (v. 34). In Israel,
this was not merely a matter of material inheritance; it had
a religious significance. This is the point of the comment in
Heb. 12.16. But the story as written in Genesis is set in the
total context of the Jacob narrative. The writer makes no
comment and certainly does not praise Jacob. Again,
nothing is said about the divine Blessing and promise. It
may well be that, as the author presents the story, he is
suggesting that some explanation of Jacob's conduct may
be found in a deep-seated resentment against the favouritism accorded to his twin (v. 28). It has often been noted that
J is acutely perceptive of psychological processes. But this
story is not told for ethical instruction any more than our
Lord's stories of the unjust steward and unrighteous judge.
Further, as the story develops, it would seem that Jacob
lost all that he had so cleverly grasped. But the divine purpose is yet to be fulfilled, even though the human agent is
of such unpromising material. This indeed is the OT presentation of Israel as the people of God (cf. Deut. 9.6).
There are historical situations in the history of Israel in
which the leaders of the nation sought to gain, and well
nigh lost, by political intrigue, what could only be received
humbly and trustfully from the Lord's hand. Against the
general background, the deep religious insight of this
teacher glows the more brightly.

## STORIES ABOUT ISAAC

## Ch. 26

As the setting of these stories shows, these derive from
the Southern tradition, and probably took their present

form at Beer-sheba. The stories themselves have close parallels with those already recorded about Abraham. The most striking similarity is between 26.1, 7-11 and 12.10-16; 20.1-18. The renewal of the promise recalls 12.2, 3, 7; 15.7; 22.17; and the well incidents 26.23-33 recall 21.31-33. It seems reasonable to suppose that we have here a variant tradition of stories otherwise related of Abraham. The motive for such duplication can only be conjectured. It may be assumed that no traditions about Isaac survived, apart from that of his marriage with Rebekah (in which, however, he plays only an incidental part), and he certainly plays no part in OT reference, except as the necessary transmitter of the divine blessing and promise from Abraham to Jacob. We note then (a) the careful enunciation of the divine promise (2-5, 24) and its fulfilment (12-16); (b) that this chapter interrupts the sequence of thought between chs. 25 and 27; (c) that it is largely a recapitulation of the temptations and trials of the man of faith in the faithful discharge of his obedience. This duplication may be seen to have purpose. The divine promise is renewed for each generation, and is full of the power of fulfilment. It requires the same trustful obedience, yet, when men fail in their response, they are recalled to their original loyalty. The life of man is at all time under the sovereign rule of God. Isaac may be a shadow of his father but his shadow is cast by the same sun upon the same ground. Repetition is a necessary part of a teacher's technique.

**1-5.** *The renewal of the promise.* The proper names, GERAR, ABIMELECH, PHILISTINES (with PHICHOL in v. 26) occur in chs. 20 and 21.22, 32, where the anachronism of Philistines in Canaan was noted. Some eighty years have elapsed from the time of the Abraham story. ABIMELECH and PHICHOL could therefore not be the same as in that story. Yet the appearance of these two names in the same circumstances, so long after the former event, supports the suggestion that

this is a variant form of the same story. Two new features
appear in this section. Isaac is not to go down to Egypt;
and Abraham is described, uniquely, as a man of outstand-
ing obedience and loyalty. The former may indicate the
gradual transition between the nomadic life of Abraham
and the more settled life of Isaac. He must live in the land
of promise, trusting God to supply his needs in that land.
But the form of the phrase in v. 2 would gain point for
those who heard the prophetic word in the eighth century
(cf. Isa. 31.1, etc.). The latter feature is without parallel
and suggests a period of reflection. Not only Abraham's
faith, but also his loyal obedience have provided the means
by which the divine blessing became operative in the life of
his descendants. In man's response to God, faith must have
priority; but real faith must issue in loyal obedience. The
thought is picked up again in v. 24, FOR MY SERVANT ABRA-
HAM'S SAKE, a phrase which recalls the frequent 'for the
sake of David' in Kings (cf. I Kings 11.32-34, etc.).

**6-11.** Isaac could not even claim the justification of Abraham's half-truth. Yet in this form of the story Rebekah is
saved from the indignity of being taken into the royal
harem. From this indignity she is saved by the 'accident'
that Abimelech saw Isaac caressing his wife (v. 8). The
word (AV SPORTING) is again a word-play on the name
Isaac, as in 17.17; 18.12-15; 21.6, 9.

**10. lightly**
   i.e. 'easily' (RSV).

**12-22.** While the main theme is the same as in 21.22-34,
the details vary. Isaac is presented as much more of a
settled dweller than was Abraham, and with sufficient
security to till the soil (v. 12). The Gentile king is jealous of
Isaac's prosperity (vv. 14, 16). Wells previously dug by
Abraham have been stopped up by the Philistines (v. 15).
Three names of springs are recorded (vv. 20-22).

**12.** Refers back to vv. 1 f. RECEIVED is literally 'found' (RV), suggesting unexpected good fortune (so also vv. 19, 32). The end of the verse offers the explanation. Wealth gained by good husbandry, not by exploitation of others, was always regarded as evidence of divine blessing.

**15.** Is a note in parenthesis and should not interrupt the sequence of thought from vv. 14-16. The Philistine intention was to prevent Isaac from encroaching on their land.

**19. springing**
AV and RVm, RSV 'living', graphically indicates the ancient attitude to water flowing up from the earth as being endowed with mysterious life. It was naturally preferred to rain water gathered in a cistern and was regarded as a direct gift of God (cf. Jer. 2.13; John 4.10, 13, 20-22). Two of the names, SITNAH and REHOBOTH, appear to have been preserved to this day. Again we are given what appear to be etymologies. More probably the names were chosen because by this means the shrine teacher would remind Israel of the way of life under God's rule. His people will meet with contention and strife but will eventually come into a large Place where there is room for peaceful expansion (cf. Ps. 4.1; 31.8, etc.).

**23-33.** *The Covenant with Abimelech* (cf. 21.22-34). The promise is renewed at the ancient shrine. Isaac's prosperity is clear evidence, even to his enemies, that God is with him, and they suddenly seek a covenant with the man of the blessing (cf. 21.22). The story presents one of those characteristic reversals of human judgment by the divine of which the most notable OT example is Isa. 52.13-53.12.

**23.** Suggests that Isaac was responsible for naming the sacred place BEER-SHEBA on account of the oath (*shib'ah*). Clearly this is a variant form of the ancient tradition with Isaac instead of Abraham as the central figure.

**34, 35.** Is a characteristic Priestly note, preparing the way for 27.46–28.9. Formally it is at variance with the intervening material, where Esau is his father's favourite. It is, in fact, a further interpretation of the faith that the Lord chose Jacob to be the inheritor of the blessing. It is not easy, however, to reconcile this with 36.1-3. It may be assumed that there were such genealogical traditions in existence in Priestly circles of post-exilic days and they were preserved without any attempt to modify them in the interests of consistency. It is remarkable that these Hittites have Semitic names. It is also to be noted that Ezekiel refers to a Hittite strain in Israel's life (Ezek. 16.3, 45). It is possible that the word used here is a word of reproach rather than of racial origin, in much the same way as the modern Englishman would use the term vandal.

## JACOB'S FRAUDULENT ACQUISITION OF THE BLESSING

### 27.1-45

This is one of the most unpleasant stories of the book of Genesis. It is the story of a man who gained his end by trickery. He got the better of his brother. It may be said that Esau deserved to lose the blessing since he had so little regarded his birthright (25.34), but this hardly justifies Jacob. Nothing, however, can excuse the deceit practised on the aged and blind Isaac, or the lies told to him by Jacob. And this story is told about the one who was to become the ancestor of Israel, the people of God! It should be noted that nothing in the story is said to condone Jacob's conduct, still less to praise him. Indeed the moving scene presented in vv. 30-40 suggests that the narrator felt a genuine pity for one so outrageously outwitted, as well as for the dying father so terribly deceived. Again, the conduct of Rebekah was such as to arouse the most vigorous

condemnation in ancient Israel. For not only did she in-
stigate this deception; she was, by her conduct, acting
against her husband and so destroying the unity of the
family. A household was a psychic community, centring on
the father; the function of a man's wife was to help in
creating and maintaining that unity. She became 'bone of
his bones and flesh of his flesh', the one adequate to make
him a whole man. That a woman should deceive her husband in any sphere was a heinous fault. It may be said that
the conduct of Rebekah and Jacob was the product of a
long-standing resentment against Isaac's favouritism of
Esau (25.28). It may also be said that they were acting to
fulfil the oracle (25.23). Neither of these excuses is suggested in the telling of the story. Such conduct could not
be justified in Israel. In fact the story ends in weakness and
failure for all concerned. The dying Isaac can give no blessing to his favourite son; the latter is condemned to a life
of hardship and peril. Jacob is compelled to leave his home,
and apparently all hope of succeeding to his inheritance.
Rebekah is parted from the son for whose sake she had
deceived her husband.

It is when we read the story as it is presented, without
any attempt to exonerate the characters of the people concerned, but in the total context of Genesis, that we can see
the significance of the story. It is a thoroughly human narrative, full of the weakness, trickery, and ruthless ambition
that marks so much of human life. It may well have been
originally one of the many popular stories which delighted
to demonstrate the superiority of Israel over Edom, reflect-
ing moral standards which the prophets condemned. That
would certainly account for the fact that *in the story*, the
great themes of Genesis—divine promise and blessing,
human faith and obedience—are ignored. But the Genesis
narrator has made his own use of the story, just because
it was so well known and popular. The ancestor of the
people of God was no ideal, heroic figure, but a man of

faults and failings like other men. It is with such men that
God in his sovereign grace has resolved to work. It is to
Jacob, who has lost everything by his own trickery, and in
his utter need that God came (28.10-22), and only from
that point does the father of Israel, the people of God, really
begin to live. There is, in fact, no human justification for
God's love for Israel. But it is in terms of that love alone
that Israel can live. Yet, though none of the human actors
in the story is aware of it, the sovereign will of God is being
fulfilled. The story appears to belong to the Southern tradition (J). A similar story may have been told in the North,
and some slight variations from that tradition may have
been included. But if so, the story has acquired a homo-
geneity in the mind of the narrator and attempts at some
analysis are not wholly convincing.

**1-5.** *Isaac and Esau.* The paternal blessing was normally
given as death approached, according to the Genesis tradition. It is part of the substance of life (soul), and before
death must be given over to the heir. The story reflects the
thought of the ancient world. In order that the blessing
may enter the soul of the heir, physical contact must be
made. In order that it should be given with strength, the
aged Isaac must be strengthened with food (v. 4). The blessing was not merely a pious wish, but an effective communication of psychic energy. With great artistry, the main
elements of the tragedy are set before us in a few words:
Isaac's blindness, his preference for Esau, the latter's passion for the hunt which had already cost him his birthright.

**6-17.** *Rebekah and Jacob.* However unworthy her purpose,
one cannot but admire the skill and devotion with which
Rebekah plans on behalf of her favourite. She thinks of
everything, food, clothing and disguise. She is even prepared to take upon herself the curse if the plan fails; and,
in view of the ancient belief in the power of the curse, this

is a tribute to her devotion to Jacob. For the curse, like the blessing, was thought to be instinct with the power of the utterer, it enters into the soul of the accursed to destroy, particularly when the soul of such a person has already been weakened by wrong-doing. One scarcely needs the explicit warning of Lev. 19.14; Deut. 27.18 (relatively late formulations of ancient teaching) to recognize the gravity of the evil being planned.

### 7. before the Lord
Lit. to Yahweh's face, in front of Yahweh. This would suggest that Isaac had some representation of Yahweh in his tent. In any case it emphasizes the solemnity of the blessing and the divine reinforcement of its power.

**10.** The importance of the blessing is that it is irrevocable, even when given in error. It has as much objective reality as a material gift and, according to ancient law preserved in the Nuzi tablets, it was legally binding. It was a last will and testament charged with the power of its own ful- filment (cf. vv. 33, 37, 41).

### 15. goodly raiment
The best clothing. The verse makes it clear that both the sons were still members of the household and un- married at the time of this incident. The note at 26.34 is not part of this tradition.

**18-29.** *Isaac and Jacob.* In this and the following scene the artistic skill reaches its highest expression; here is the build- ing up of suspense, there is the pathos. It begins with a blatant lie (v. 19) which is reinforced by a blasphemous explanation of his unexpected appearance so soon after Isaac's request (v. 20), 'Yahweh thy God has given me success'. The father's suspicions are lulled by the feel of the skin and the familiar smell of the hunter attaching to the clothes.

**23. so he blessed him**

Anticipates vv. 27 ff. Probably this is an indication of the welding together of the two traditions.

**25.** To take food and drink from another is to establish a relationship of soul. The blessing 27b-29 is in rhythmic form characteristic of prophetic oracles. Characteristically, too, it is brought to expression by a sense-experience (smell) which leads into the opening words of the blessing. It is to be noted however that it is not the divine promise to Abraham and Isaac which is uttered (cf. 28.3 f.), and further that the blessing is appropriate to the settled life (Jacob/Israel) and not that of the nomadic hunter (Esau). It speaks of a fertile land to be possessed and of dominion over other nations (especially Moab, Ammon and Edom). The story represents Isaac as uttering a prophetic word which was in fact fulfilled in the days of David, some five hundred years later. Immediately, however, Jacob must flee the land thus promised and go in fear of Esau over whom he is given dominion.

**28. dew of heaven**

During the hot, dry summer Palestine is dependent on the heavy night-dew for the growth of the crops.

**30-40.** *Isaac and Esau.* The intensely dramatic nature of this scene is presented with fine artistry: the simple confidence of the returned hunter, the shock to Isaac, the discovery of Jacob's deception, the impossibility of recalling the blessing, the despair of Esau when he finds that he has lost everything.

**36. Jacob . . . supplanted**

(cf. 25.26). BIRTHRIGHT . . . BLESSING, the two words are very similar in Hebrew: *Bekorathi . . . Birkathi.*

GENESIS 27.39-45 81

**39.** Isaac's 'last word' to Esau is also rhythmic in form, and many of the same words are used as in his blessing of Jacob; but it is all with opposite effect. It is the more pointed in that the opening preposition in Hebrew can be translated either as 'a part of' (v. 28) or 'apart from' (v. 39) so we should render v. 39 f.

> Behold! away from the earth's fatness
>     shall thy dwelling be,
>     and away from the dew of heaven above.
> And by thy sword thou shalt live; and thou shalt serve
>     thy brother
> And it shall come to pass that when thou shalt become
>     restless
> Thou shalt break off his yoke from upon thy neck.

This is clearly not a blessing, but a curse. Esau is condemned to live in an infertile land (Edom), providing food only for the roving hunter. The word of hope expressed in the last clause suggests a time after David's subjugation of Edom, when at various times Edom was able to assert its independence (cf. II Kings 8.20).

**41-45.** *Rebekah and Jacob.* Rebekah, fearful of the wrath of Esau towards Jacob, warns the latter to flee to her brother's home in Haran. Had Esau killed Jacob, he would be put to death as a punishment so that Rebekah would have been left a childless widow, a grim fate for a woman in that society. We are left with a feeling of astonishment that such a story (and that of 25.21-34) should have been told of the ancestor of Israel. Clearly the great teachers of Israel were no starry-eyed idealists. Rather do they insist that in the midst of human intrigue and treachery, even when the consequences, ruin and failure, have come upon man, God is at work for the fulfilment of his great purposes. The very evil that Israel has brought about will be for discipline.

F

## JACOB SENT TO LABAN (P)

### 27.46–28.9

It is clear that we have here an entirely different interpretation of the traditional story of Jacob's journey to the
home of his mother's kinsmen, and of Isaac's blessing.
Since Isaac lived in Southern Canaan, his sons would normally marry women of Canaanite families. Esau has
already so married, greatly to the distress of Rebekah. Isaac
sends Jacob to the family from which his own wife had
come and freely blesses him, with the great words of the
divine blessing. Jacob is to be in the true line of succession
from Abraham. Vocabulary, style and point of view make
clear that we have here the interpretation of Israel's origins
that owes its origin to the profound reflection of the Jerusalem priests of exilic or post-exilic days.[1] It is one of the
distinctive qualities of Biblical faith that it is capable of
new expression to meet the profound change of historical
circumstance. In the exile and in post-exilic days the Jews
could only maintain their integrity, and with that the distinctive nature of their religion, by refusing to intermingle
with other peoples. This is not what modern man means by
'racial segregation'. It corresponds more nearly to the
peculiar difficulties confronting the Church when it is a
minority group. The issue is made clear in Neh. 13.23-29.
Thus the Priestly writer makes use of the ancient traditions
to relate the faith to the new situation.

This is the point of view in this section. But when it is
read within the total context of the Jacob story as we now
have it in Genesis, a further consideration arises. The sin
of man appears to have destroyed any possibility of the
fulfilment of the divine promise to Abraham. Isaac is at

[1] See Alan Richardson, *Genesis I–XI*, Torch Bible Commentaries, SCM
Press, London, 1953, pp. 22 ff.

the point of death (27.1-5); Rebekah's treachery and Jacob's lies have compelled the latter to flee from the land of promise (27.41-45); Esau cannot be blessed (27.30-40) and has gone outside the sacred community (26. 34, 35; 27.46). What hope is there? The answer is that in all this God is at work to bring about his fulfilment. It was, after all, not Esau's wrath but God's will that Jacob should go to Laban, where he will renew the family.

**46. daughters of Heth**

i.e. Hittite women (cf. 26.34, 35).

**multitude**

The word is usually translated 'congregation' and lies behind the NT word for 'Church'.

**28.4 the blessing of Abraham**

(cf. 25.6-8). WHEREIN THOU ART A STRANGER render 'of thy sojournings' (AVm, RV, RSV).

## JACOB'S DREAM AT BETHEL

### 28.10-22

This is the continuation of 27.45. In flight from Beer-sheba Jacob arrives at a place where, against all his ex-pectation, God meets him and he receives a renewal of the Promise given to Abraham (12.3, 7; 13.14-16). Jacob recog-nizes that the PLACE is the house of God (BETH-EL) and so names it. He then solemnly dedicates himself to the ser-vice of the Lord.

The primary interest of the story is in the origin of BETH-EL as a sacred place in Israelite tradition. Throughout the monarchy period this was an important cult centre for the Northern Kingdom from the time of Jeroboam I (I

Kings 12.29). It was of course a Canaanite sanctuary before
that; excavations indicate that its history goes back to
about 2000 BC; it was destroyed in the latter part of the
thirteenth century (cf. Judg. 1.22-25) and was slowly rebuilt.
As a royal sanctuary it flourished and is referred to by
Amos and Hosea in the eighth century BC (Amos 3.14, etc.;
Hos. 12.4 and also, as Beth-Aven, Hos. 4.15 etc.). It was
destroyed by Josiah (II Kings 23.15). Beyond the fact of its
pre-Israelite existence as a cult centre nothing is known in
detail. The name Beth-el suggests that its cult was associated with the Canaanite god El, known from the Ras
Shamra tablets as the head of the pantheon. The story,
then, was originally one associated with that cult-centre.
It is therefore, at one level, one of those stories which show
how the God of Israel assumed to himself the powers and
functions earlier attributed to the Canaanite God, and thus
manifested his sovereignty over the land where El was worshipped. It appears to derive mainly from the Northern
tradition although there are indications that a similar story
preserved in the south has been associated with it (J, vv.
13-16, 19: the main story is E). Thus the cult story would
conserve the association of the sanctuary with the patriarch
Jacob, be a constant reminder that this was a place of
revelation, and establish the claim to receive tithes from
all Israel (v. 22).

But the inclusion of this story in Genesis raises further
questions. Why was this story preserved by those for whom
BETH-EL had become a place associated with the sin of
Jeroboam and so destroyed by the reformer King (II Kings
23.15)? Why was it included in the Torah of post-exilic
days? The answer may be found by reading the story
against the background of the Jewish people who had been
taken into exile, far from the land where they had known
and worshipped God. It was against all popular belief that
a god should be present and active away from his acknowledged territory. Yet even far from their homeland THE

LORD IS IN THIS PLACE AND I KNEW IT NOT. It was one of the
great contributions of the priest-prophet Ezekiel to know
and declare this. How better to fix this great faith in the
mind of the people of God than to include this well-known
and often repeated tradition in those tragic circumstances!
Further, there is contained in the story a hope of a return
and the confidence that the future, however dark and unknown, is in the hand of the Lord. Thus, when the external
circumstances of the life of God's people appeared hope-
less, faith was reborn and maintained by the telling of this
ancient story of the patriarch. The presence and activity of
God is assured, not because his people deserve it, but
because he has declared his promise and will fulfil it.

### 10. Jacob

in leaving BEER-SHEBA would assume that he was leaving
the shrine of his father's God.

### 11. lighted upon

Humanly speaking it was by chance that he came to the
PLACE; that is emphasized by the Hebrew verb; A CERTAIN
PLACE, literally ' the place ' and especially ' the sacred place '
(cf. 22.3 f.). It had of course associations with Abraham
(12.8; 13.3), but this appears to be unknown to Jacob. It
was some twelve miles north of Jerusalem. The fact that
it was an ancient Canaanite sanctuary must, however, have
been apparent, but Jacob would have no knowledge of the
god worshipped there. The name of the god may well have
been Beth-el (cf. 31.13; 35.7, notes), and a god by the name
continued to be worshipped in Jeremiah's day (cf. Jer.
48.13) and by the Jewish refugees of the fifth century BC at
Elephantine in Egypt.

### 12. ladder

This is the only occurrence of the word in the OT, but
it is known from other semitic language as well as from a

similar Hebrew word (cf. II Sam. 20.15; II Kings 19.32, etc., 'a bank'). It means rather a stairway apparently resembling a Babylonian ziggurat or temple-tower. The existence of some such structure at the sacred place produced the form of Jacob's dream. This stairway was 'the bank between heaven and earth', up and down which God's 'messengers' (ANGELS) pass continually to carry out his commands. This receives a new content of meaning for Jacob, as he receives the revelation of the God of Abraham and Isaac and his call; the great Promise is renewed for him (vv. 13-16 J).

### 13. above it

This could, and perhaps should, be rendered 'beside him', i.e. bending over him as he slept. He recognizes the supreme sanctity of this place (THE GATE OF HEAVEN) and pledges his life to the service of him who has made himself known (vv. 17-22 (E)).

### 17. dreadful

A word characteristic of the Psalms and expressive of the deep awe that fills the soul of man in the evident presence of God.

### 18. the stone

This serves to explain the origin of the pillar or sacred monolith (rendered seventeen times 'image' in AV) the erection of which was forbidden in the later religion (Ex. 23.24). Such objects were common in many parts of the world as well as in Canaan and regarded as the god's dwelling place (v. 22). The act of anointing is to acknowledge its peculiar sanctity and to dedicate it to the god.

**19.** Apparently Luz was the name of the city and it is still referred to by that name in Josh. 16.2; Judg. 1.23, 26, and Beth-el the sanctuary name. The religious significance of the latter replaced the name of the city.

**20-22.** The vow was not a bargain. It is a recognition of a new relationship implicit in the revelation and an obligation on Jacob's part to render thanksgiving as the divine blessing takes effect.

**22.** The practice of tithing was a recognized feature of the Beth-el sanctuary (cf. Amos 4.4).

## JACOB AND LABAN

### Chs. 29-31

Once again we are in the realm of popular story-telling, the normal way in the East of preserving traditions of the past. It is in no sense a biography of Jacob; the incidents recorded in detail are few for the span of twenty years. They are such incidents as would gain a firm hold on popular imagination. At our level it is a story of a long contest between two very clever tricksters, in which Jacob proves successful. It is told with all the rough humour characteristic of a relatively primitive people. And everyone would be aware of the constant struggle of political Israel to get the better of her neighbour. Another motif in this story is Jacob's love for Rachel, a fine redeeming factor in an otherwise unscrupulous character. Yet another is that of the rivalry between the sister-wives (the Hebrew word for a second wife meant rival!), and this pathetic account of the unloved yet faithful elder wife. The Jacob of this story is not very different from the man who tricked his brother. There is nothing explicitly religious in such a story, in spite of occasional references to God. Yet, as this story now appears, we are increasingly aware that the events of the story have a deeper significance than is apparent to the characters in it. Yahweh, the God of Abraham, Isaac and now Jacob is at work in this far away place,

preparing the man he has chosen to fulfil his role in the
drama of history. It is he who gives or withholds sons to
Jacob, prosperity in an unpromising situation and the
signal to return to his native land. The point is made, with
great artistic skill: 31.13, with its recalling to Jacob of
the great moment of revelation, and 31.42, with its recollection of the ever-faithful God, present and active with Jacob.
In this down to earth, even unedifying and certainly very
human series of events, God is at work to fulfil his purpose
in creating a people for himself.

(It is possible to recognize the weaving together of various strands in the story as we now have it. Tribal interests
and history are reflected in the children of the two wives
and their handmaids. But this is an entirely natural process in which ancient traditions preserved in more than
one part of Israel have been gathered together into a continuous narrative.)

## JACOB'S MEETING WITH HIS KINSFOLK

### 29.1-14

Nothing is told about the long journey from Beth-el; that
had no significance for the author. What is important is that
he came to THE LAND OF THE PEOPLE OF THE EAST. This
phrase is difficult. It is hardly appropriate to Haran in Aram-
Naharaim, which could hardly be described as other than
north of Canaan. It is in fact slightly east of north, but its
distance—some 300 miles—would make the description
'Easterners' quite inappropriate. Further it only took
Jacob, moving with his flock and herds, ten days to reach
the hill country of Gilead from Laban's territory (31.22, 23).
This would be quite impossible. It is true that Jacob's
destination in 28.5, 10 is in this Mesopotamian district, but
that belongs to a different cycle of tradition. It is also true

that in 31.18 PADAN-ARAM is noted as the home of Laban,
but this is a much later note (P), serving to link this story
with the note in 28.1-9. In the earlier form of the story,
Laban's shepherds describe themselves as OF HARAN (29.4).
The apparent contradiction may in fact reflect the actual
historical situation. The Aramaean people, at one time
settled around Haran, did for a time extend further south
and east into Mesopotamia and later were driven back into
the Syrian desert whence subsequently, from the eleventh
century, many settled in city states of which Damascus was
the best known. The situation described in this part of the
Jacob story clearly reflects a period during which the
Aramaean tribes were in the Syrian desert and before the
more permanent settlement of this people. It should occasion no surprise that their original location in Haran was a
living part of their tradition (29.4). The setting of this whole
story is that of a desert oasis.

**2 f.** The tenses of the verbs need to be rendered as imper-
fects ' used to water ', ' used to be gathered ', ' used to roll ',
etc.

**4-6** describes a typical scene when a stranger meets an unknown body of nomads. It is essential for him to suggest a
kinship. In the phrase IS HE WELL we have the Hebrew
word *shalom*, an inquiry about his total welfare and prosperity. Rachel means ' ewe '.

**7, 8.** refers to a recognized custom with the force of law.
Several clans have right of access to the well, so the well
was only used when all were present in order that no suspicion of improper use by any one should arise.

**9, 10.** The arrival of Rachel, however, prompts Jacob to
take action, even though it infringed the local custom. In
fact he moved the stone which normally required a number

of men. There seems to be here and in 28.18; 32.25 f. a tradition that Jacob was a man of superhuman strength. But this theme is not otherwise pursued. In this passage we have the beginning of the one great romance (as the Western reader would understand it) in the book of Genesis.

**12-14.** The all-important matter of kinship was established by a brief recital of family relationships. Jacob is a near kinsman (BROTHER) of Laban, and is therefore assured of his hospitality and protection.

## THE MARRIAGE TO LEAH AND RACHEL

### 29.15-30

It is quite obvious that Jacob did not tell Laban of the circumstances under which he left home in ch. 27, and he is treated as an honoured guest. The fact that no mention is made of any son of Laban at this part of the story may suggest that Laban, in lieu of a male heir, was acquiring a son by marrying his daughters to him. But if subsequently sons were born to Laban then they would feel that their heritage was jeopardized (31.1). It was entirely appropriate that Laban should wish to retain the services of this skilled shepherd and offer appropriate recompense. Jacob asks for Rachel and offers his services for seven years as the suitable bride-price (see note on 24.53). It was of course, an extravagant offer, but if the marriage included an expectation of eventual inheritance, not entirely disinterested.

**17. Leah**
i.e. Wild cow. TENDER EYED—her eyes were weak, a very serious blemish to the mind of the Oriental. Rachel was beautiful and lovely.

**19.** The marriage of first-cousins (cf. Isaac and Rebekah) was regarded as the ideal; such unions would strengthen the family, while marriages between members of totally unrelated clans tended to disrupt the family.

**23.** The bride was heavily veiled. The mention of the banquet is quite deliberate. Thus the trickster was himself shamelessly tricked and the explanation offered by Laban in v. 26 cannot be taken seriously. Whatever truth there might be in it, he had in fact contracted to give his younger daughter in marriage, and such an 'explanation' should have preceded the contract. Yet as the story is told there is surely a subtle reminder of the conflict between the elder and younger brothers, in which Jacob had shamelessly tricked Esau of his rights. The marriage could not now be repudiated, and if Jacob still wished to marry Rachel, he must bind himself to Laban for a further seven years. Deeper than all this was the fact that though Jacob had no intention of marrying Leah, it was in fact from this union that Judah derived, the tribe from which the Lord's anointed, David, should come.

**24.** is a parenthetic note interrupting the sequences of thought (so also v. 29); it is intended to prepare the mind of the reader for the events of the following chapters and may be ascribed to the Priestly editor; HANDMAID—a female slave.

## JACOB'S CHILDREN

### 29.31–30.24

In the birth and naming of the children of Jacob we can recognize the influences of the subsequent history of the people of Israel. This is further explicated in the blessing of

Jacob (ch. 49). Here, the point is made that the neglected
wife had the greater blessing from God, while the favoured
wife was for a long while childless. Throughout the narrative, the recollection of many ancient customs and beliefs
has been faithfully preserved. The 'explanations' attached
to the names should not be regarded as etymological but, as
commonly, produced by assonance. This kind of word play
was more highly regarded by the ancient Israelites than by
us; indeed if a favourable word play could be produced it
was held to ensure good fortune.

### 31. hated
Less loved (cf. Deut. 21.15 ff.; Matt. 6.24).

### 32. Reuben
sounds like 'see a son' (*re'u ben*) but is somewhat im-
probably linked with 'has seen my affliction' (*rā'āh be'onyi*).

### 33. Simeon
suggests the sound of *shāma'* 'has heard'.

### 34. Levi
suggests *lāwāh* 'has joined' but the word is also known
as a term for 'priest'.

### 35. Judah
(*yehûdāh*) suggests *yādāh*—'gave thanks'.

**30.1 f.** To be childless was to be regarded as under divine
displeasure, for only God, the Source of life, could give
children.

**3.** Describes what appears to be an ancient rite of adoption.

### 6. Dan
suggests the verb *dān* 'he has judged'. It should be

remembered that to judge includes the meaning 'do what is right for' and so to restore one who has been wrongly afflicted (cf. Ps. 26.1).

**8. Naphtali**

suggests the noun *naphtûlē* 'wrestlings of' and the verb *niphtalti* 'I have wrestled' (the word literally means 'twisted' as in Prov. 8.8, AV 'forward', RSV 'twisted').

**9-13.** Rachel's action somewhat unnecessarily prompts Leah to a similar procedure, and by her slave Jacob has two further sons, GAD (fortune) and ASHER (be happy).

**14-21.** This little story seems rather awkwardly introduced in connection with Leah's next two sons and a daughter. Almost certainly it was originally (in folk story) connected with Rachel's giving birth to Joseph (vv. 22-24). It may be supposed that the teller of the story as we have it either deliberately omitted it in favour of the more genuinely religious account of Joseph's birth, or deliberately modified it to the same end. The former is probably the right explanation since vv. 17-23 are in the main from the Northern traditions.

**14. Reuben**

is still apparently a child. WHEAT HARVEST—about May in this part of the world. MANDRAKES—*mandragora officinarum*, a plant of the same family as the tomato, potato and belladonna, whose yellow fruit was believed to have aphrodisiac qualities and also thought to promote conception. The Hebrew name is connected with the word for 'beloved' in Isa. 5.1.

**16. Surely I have hired thee**

Hebrew: *sākōr sekartikā*.

**18. my hire**

= *sekāri*. The words suggest the name Issachar (Hebrew
*yissakar*). There is a double word play on this name; one
connects it with Leah's giving the mandrakes to Rachel, the
other with her giving her female slave to Jacob. The name
is thus given the meaning ' hireling '.

**20. Zebulun**

also is connected with two words, *zābad* ' endow ' and
*zābal* ' maintain ', ' nourish ' (AV) RV, ' dwell with ', RSV,
' honour ', deriving the word from Ugaritic and suggesting
that the name ZEBULUN means ' the princely one '.

**21. Dinah**

The one daughter mentioned by name (others are referred
to at 37.35) is given without explanation. It is connected
with Dan. Does this suggest the history of the Danite tribe,
too weak to maintain itself in its original settlement close
to Philistine territory and finding security as it migrated
northwards? (cf. Judg. 13.2-25 with 18.27-29 and 5.17). It
should be noted that some of these names appear in extra-
Biblical texts of the first half of the second millennium BC
as tribal names, some in various parts of Canaan.

**22. remembered**

To remember someone, in Biblical thought, is to receive
that person's being into one's life so that appropriate action
is taken. Remembering is not merely a mental activity, it
involves the total life of him who remembers.

**23 f.** The name JOSEPH is associated with two verbs, *yāsaph*
—to gather or take away, and *'asaph*—to add; the latter
expresses the prayer that God will add another son, a
hope that is subsequently fulfilled in the birth of Benjamin
(35.17 f.).

## Jacob's Wealth

### 30.25-43

Just as a numerous progeny was regarded as the working out of the Blessing, so also is success in husbandry and, negatively, the futility of hostility against the man of the Blessing. Again the story is presented in thoroughly human terms, but in such a way that the reader will recognize that the Lord God of Israel is working for the fulfilment of his purpose. Jacob wishes to return home, and it is the divine purpose that this man should so return with his family to the land of promise. Again we read of a contest in cunning, but this time Jacob outwits his father-in-law. We can imagine the pleasure with which such a story would be recounted among the shepherds of a later date; similar stories abound in such communities. No attempt is made by the Genesis writer to moralize or draw pious comments. It is only as we read this in its larger context that we recognize that even in this situation God is at work. Jacob is not commended, but he must return to Canaan showing the evidence of the divine choice.

The details of this passage are sometimes confusing and there appear to be repetitions that hold up the story. The latter may simply be a device of the story-teller (as distinct from the writer); the former may indicate how the story has developed into its present unity from a story told with minor variations in various groups. The difficulties will be indicated in the notes.

**25 f.** Characteristically in terms of Oriental custom, Jacob makes no mention of any payment for his services; but it would be a serious loss of honour if Laban made no adequate offer. Then the bargaining begins!

**27.** First Laban courteously acknowledges the benefit he has received from Jacob's services. There is no word to correspond to TARRY (AV, RV) in the Hebrew. It is a good example of the story-telling form where the audience silently supplies a necessary verb. I HAVE LEARNED BY EXPERIENCE—the Hebrew word means 'to divine' by consulting omens (cf. RV, RSV, and 44.5, 15). It is an implied compliment to Jacob by a recognition of the superior power of Jacob's God. So Laban offers to recompense Jacob (v. 28). Jacob proceeds to underline the value of his past services, and makes it clear that it is now time for him to be looking after his own affairs (v. 30). Again Laban makes what sounds like an open offer. Behind all this diplomatic courtesy we can recognize that both men are on their guard. On the one hand, Laban does not wish to lose Jacob's services; yet he cannot insist on his remaining since Jacob is a kinsman and no slave. On the other hand Jacob is not on very secure ground; he might justly claim recompense, but it was by no means certain that he could legally take his wives and family from Laban's clan (cf. 31.43). And since he was in Laban's territory, he certainly could not take them and the flocks without Laban's consent. All this was known to both parties, although of course neither mentioned it! So Jacob's reply that he would ask for no wages was not understood by either party to be taken literally. Laban's honour as a sheikh could not permit that. In fact Jacob asks for what at first sounds like a very modest reward, and offers a further period of service. In that part of the world sheep were nearly always white and goats black (sheep's wool was a simile for whiteness—Isa. 1.18; Cant. 4.2; goats for blackness, Cant. 4.1). To this Laban at once agrees, all the more that when those selected for Jacob are set apart, it would be easy to see whether Jacob was being straight with him (v. 33). It is evident that Laban is still suspicious, since Jacob's flock is removed from Laban's by a three-days' journey.

Now comes the point of Jacob's offer of further service.
Acting on the belief that the offspring will be marked by
what the ewes see at the time of conception, he ensures that
his own flock will be greatly increased. That such a belief
has no foundation in fact is beside the point. It was accepted
without question by the hearers of the story (and still per-
sists). A derisive touch also appears in the repeated word
WHITE in v. 37 (Hebrew 'lābān'). The reason for choosing
these three trees is not obvious, though POPLAR (Hebrew
libneh) again points to Laban.

**40.** Is difficult since the flock under Jacob's care had been
separated from those selected as his property (v. 36). We
can only suggest the inclusion of a variant tradition. The
main point of the story remains unaffected.

**41.** Describes an extension of the trick; only the stronger
animals received this treatment. So the number and the
vigour of the striped, speckled and spotted were increased
to Jacob's advantage. Laban has accepted the bargain and
it cannot be revoked. The second round has been decisively
won by Jacob.

## JACOB'S DEPARTURE

### 31.1-54

**1-18.** *Preparations.*   **19-25.** *Laban's pursuit.*
**26-55.** *The Covenant.*

This part of the story also existed in two forms with
minor variations, though the main narrative follows that
from the Northern tradition. Once again it is a story of
trickery, a contest of wits which is finally decisive in favour
of Jacob. The popular appeal of such a story for the

Israelites is obvious enough. But the reader is more aware
than ever of the over-ruling activity of God. Neither the
hostility of Laban, nor the panic flight of Jacob which so
nearly ended in disaster (v. 29), could prevent the fulfilment of the divine purpose.

Evidence for the variant traditions may be found in the
double reason given for Jacob's flight (vv. 1 and 3 (J) and
2 and 13 (E)) and the double account of GALEED and
MIZPAH in vv. 45-54. The narrative also includes a brief
note in v. 18 from (P). It is to be noted that Jacob appears
in a much more favourable light in this narrative. The increase of his wealth is directly attributed to God (vv. 7 ff.)
and the theft of the teraphim is the work of Rachel
(19.32-35). While this is obviously a story about individuals,
it reflects many features of the historical rivalry between
Israel and Syria.

**1.** Laban's sons, apparently born after Jacob's marriage
with Leah and Rachel, are naturally resentful of Jacob's
wealth at the expense of their anticipated inheritance. If the
marriage included an adoption by Laban, Jacob had certain
rights of inheritance, but the true sons could claim some
advantages (see v. 7).

**2.** Laban had good reason to be dissatisfied with the events
of the last six years (30.32-42).

**4.** Jacob, in fulfilment of his terms of service, cannot leave
the flocks. His words to Leah and Rachel (vv. 5-13) are
necessary since he must be sure of their willingness to go
with him. To have taken them against their will would
apparently have been illegal (v. 43). A form of marriage was
known among the Semites in which the wife still remained
as a member of her father's household (Judg. 14.1–15.2).

**5. hath been with me**
The Hebrew verb 'to be' is much stronger than the

English; it means 'has been present and active'. This is
what explains vv. 7 ff. In these verses the explanation is
quite different from 30.32-42 (J). The spotted and the
striped animals are successively consequent upon a change
in the terms of service, and their birth is directly attributed
to divine action.

**13.** Can only be translated 'the god Bethel', i.e. BETH-EL is
in apposition and not a genitive, and is a proper name (cf.
28.11). The verse specifically refers to Jacob's experience in
ch. 28, and it is to be inferred that the stone was regarded
as indwelt by the god Beth-el. Such a thought could not be
tolerated in orthodox Israelite belief, though it persisted
in popular thought, and the name normally has its rather
weakened significance 'House of God'. It is a remarkable
fact that the original form appears here, and it is evidence
both of the antiquity of the tradition and the faithfulness
with which it was recorded.

**14.** Rachel and Leah declare themselves as belonging to
Jacob, since their father had, by his treatment of them,
given up all rights over them. This establishes Jacob's legal
position.

**15. strangers**
Defines their legal status as members of another clan.

**19.** The spring shearing was an occasion at which the
shepherds would be very busy, and would end with a feast
(I Sam. 25.2, 11; II Sam. 13.23). IMAGES more exactly 'the
teraphim'. These were a special kind of image which not
only provided oracles (Ezek. 21.21), but according to
ancient law (Nuzi) ensured the possessor of the family inheritance. That is why Laban was more indignant about
this loss than any other (v. 30). Clearly Rachel had learned
much from her father!

**20. stole away unawares**

lit. ' stole the heart of ', i.e. ' deceived '. The heart in Hebrew thought is the seat of understanding (so v. 26).

**21. the river**

When the word stands by itself it would normally stand for the Euphrates. So in RV the word is given a capital letter, and RSV interprets as Euphrates. This may well have been in the mind of the writer and would be consistent with the Priestly note in v. 18. But the rest of the story fits the Syrian district in the neighbourhood of Damascus, and the ten days' journey to the hill country of Gilead with flocks and herds makes Euphrates impossible. It may be that in the original telling, THE RIVER referred to Abana or Pharpar (II Kings 5.12), about 100 miles from the Gilead border. Gilead was east of the Jordan, extending from the Yarmuk to the vale of Heshbon, and divided by the Jabbok gorge; that is, a district approximately equivalent to Gad and East Manasseh, but it often refers to a smaller part of the whole. It was very fertile and frequently disputed territory.

**23. brethren**

Members of the clan (so vv. 25, 32, 37, 46, 54).

**24. good or bad**

cf. 24.50.

**25.** the name of Jacob's ' mountain ' (or hill district) has disappeared from the story. It may have been the Mizpah referred to in v. 49, an obviously common name for a hill from its meaning (place of watching).

**26-30.** The argument reaches its climax in the accusation that Jacob has stolen the teraphim (cf. v. 19). The earlier stages, in which Laban represents himself as the injured party, has some justification (though Leah and Rachel cast doubts upon its sincerity, vv. 14-16), and Jacob does not really contest it. Certainly the father of this household, quite apart from emotional considerations, had an obligation towards the dependent members. In a strange land what guarantee had he that the daughters and their children would be protected? V. 27 does however suggest that he protested too much.

**30.** might be rendered, 'But now you *have* gone because you greatly desired . . .' Laban will accept that, but now comes to the real charge.

**31 f.** Jacob explains his conduct but fiercely repudiates the charge. Unwittingly he puts his favourite wife in jeopardy, from which she escapes by trickery of the worst kind.

**34. furniture**
Part of the saddle.

**36-42.** Since the charge appears to be groundless, Laban is in the wrong and Jacob in turn accuses him first of making a pretext for a mean search, and follows this up by representing him as having displayed meanness in all their relationship. This was a serious 'loss of face' for Laban.

**36. chode with**
Render: 'charged' (in a legal sense).

**42. fear of Isaac**
This phrase which occurs only here and in v. 53 apparently represents a divine name comparable to the Might of Jacob (49.24) and the Holy of Israel (Isa. 1.4, etc.). It should be spelt with a capital letter 'the Fear of Isaac'.

**43 ff.** In what follows, the individual character of the story is overshadowed by the history of relations between the Aramaeans (Nahor) and the Israelites (Jacob). Gilead was

part of the disputed territory between these two peoples.
There was a treaty, more or less honoured, which regarded
the hill country in the northern part of Gilead as the frontier. That is what gives especial point to Amos 1.3.

## 45 f. Jacob

But both v. 51 and the terms of the contract in vv. 48-50,
52 require that it should be LABAN. Possibly Laban set up
the PILLAR (standing stone) and Jacob the cairn or *vice
versa*. The material is much condensed. The meal on the
cairn was understood as uniting the souls of the contracting parties in closest proximity to the god. Very properly
in an 'international' treaty the language of each party is
used (v. 47) and the god of each nation is invoked (v. 53).
The Aramaic and the Hebrew words have the same meaning. The Hebrew is then attached to the place-name, Gilead,
another play on words which has no etymological justification.

**49.** seems a curiously intrusive verse. It may be that it
derives from one tradition in which this name rather than
Gilead appeared. This is supported by the fact that Mizpah
not only recalls the Hebrew word for WATCH (*Mispāh—
sāpāh*) but also the word for PILLAR (*massebah*). Thus God
is witness to the agreement and will observe any breach of
it, and take appropriate action. In v. 53 the verb JUDGE is
plural; the phrase GOD OF THEIR FATHERS is absent from
some Hebrew MSS. and the early Greek translation. The
position of the words in the Hebrew (following US) makes
it clear that it is a late gloss; a scholar's note identifying
the two gods referred to, Abraham's god and Nahor's god.

**54.** A sacrificial meal (probably 'peace offering') was the
proper conclusion of such a covenant whereby the life of
the two parties were bound together.

## The Arrival at Mahanaim

### 31.55–32.2

31.55 EVV is 32.1 in the Hebrew Bible. This curious note is perhaps introduced here as a deliberate interlude between the Jacob in Syria, and the Jacob in Canaan stories. It may be assumed that there was a longer story about MAHANAIM, to account for its name, and of this we have only the two verses. Echoes also appear at 32.10 TWO BANDS (*mahanoth*) and 32.21 COMPANY (*mahaneh*). MAHANAIM was a town in the territory of Gilead. The references to the divine messengers (ANGELS 28.12), the fact that Ish-bosheth was crowned there (II Sam. 2.8 f.) and that it was a Levitical city (Josh. 21.38) suggests that it was a sanctuary or cult centre. It was close to the JABBOK (v. 22) and near the JORDAN (v. 10). Thus it was well inside what was later regarded as the territory of Israel. This seems to be the significance of the story for Genesis. Jacob is to know himself within that land in which God has chosen to be with his people.

## The Reconciliation between Jacob and Esau

### Chs. 32, 33

This is the conclusion of the first part of the Jacob story, the end of his strife with his twin brother, the end of his wanderings outside the land of promise brought about by his trickery, and the beginning of a Jacob who is to become Israel. The story of the reconciliation shows a fine psychological understanding of the working of a guilty soul which suspects every act of the offended party. The story of the strange encounter with the river god (32.24-32) is formally an intrusion, but its inclusion prepares the mind for a profound theological understanding of Jacob/Israel.

## JACOB PREPARES FOR THE ENCOUNTER WITH ESAU

### 32.3-23

Since Esau was already settled in Edom (33.16) there would appear no necessity for this meeting on geographical grounds. The necessity is presented in terms of personal relationships; a reconciliation must be effected, and it can only come from the offended party. Jacob has returned with great possessions; yet everything is in jeopardy until Esau's hostility is brought to an end. It is understandable that Jacob could not believe in Esau's generosity. The first act is to send messengers to Esau in Edom. The message is couched in the language appropriate from an inferior to a superior, MY LORD, THY SERVANT (v. 4), FIND GRACE, i.e. 'gain thy favour' (v. 5). The messengers return with the news that Esau was coming to meet him with four hundred men (v. 6). This could be a mark of honour, or it could be regarded as a hostile act (TO MEET THEE, the Hebrew verb often has this hostile sense of preparing for battle, cf. the English 'encounter'). Jacob prepares for the worst.

**7 f.** The first act is to divide his possessions in the hope that at least one might escape (AV, BANDS, COMPANY, should be rendered 'camp' (*mahaneh*) and so also BANDS in v. 10. The association with v. 2 is apparently deliberate).

**9-12.** Jacob's prayer is in fact a recollection of the relationship which God has made with him. In his extremity he has no other hope.

**10. mercies . . . truth**
These are the great covenant words 'steadfast love .
faithfulness' (RSV).

**11. the mother with the children**
i.e. the whole people.

**13. thou**
The word is very emphatic in the Hebrew sentence, as
if to say 'It is thou who hast said and for that reason the
word cannot fail'. It is not so much an attempt to persuade
God, as a reminder to himself. Jacob is still the careful
schemer, but he is beginning to learn of a Power beyond
his scheming. Then follows (vv. 13-21) a further account
of an attempt to appease the supposedly hostile Esau, the
sending of a series of gifts. This is bribery, but not only so.
For if one accepts a gift from another a relationship is
created. This was perhaps more apparent in ancient modes
of thought than to modern man. A gift is an extension of
the giver's soul; to receive it meant to receive that soul
into one's own.

**20, 21.** A five-fold repetition of the Hebrew word *pānîm*
which is clearly intended to relate to vv. 30, 31, PENIEL and
to 33.10. The English words are APPEASE (cover the face),
BEFORE ME (to my face), HIS FACE, ME (my face), BEFORE HIM
(upon his face).

**22. ford Jabbok**
Read 'ford of the Jabbok'. The Jabbok is a tributary of
the Jordan and divides the district of Gilead. For the last
25 miles of its course it runs through a deep gorge to reach
the Jordan some 25 miles north of the Dead Sea. The ford
referred to here was apparently the one that is some 3 miles
east of the Jordan.

## THE WRESTLING

### 32.24-32

This is one of the most difficult stories in the Jacob saga.
It should be observed that many of the difficulties felt by a
present-day reader would not be apparent to the teller of
this story. Perhaps our difficulties mainly arise either from
an attempt to rationalize the story, which is hardly possible;
or to turn it into an allegory, which raises more difficulties
than it solves. Our difficulty is not lessened by the fact
that similar stories of wrestling with a divine being appear
in many parts of the world. Yet this story is told with a
quite remarkable economy of language and is quite unfor-
gettable. We note that the story is linked with a place-name
which by its very form suggests an ancient cult centre. It is
also linked with a dietary law (which is not otherwise mentioned in the Law), a taboo on eating the sciatic muscle.
Thirdly it is related to the giving to Jacob of a new name,
ISRAEL, which is, to our mind, most unnaturally interpreted.
These appear to be earlier interpretations of the story.
Again the word for WRESTLE is nowhere else used in the
Bible and has obviously been chosen for its similarity in
sound to JABBOK. Also, though this must not be pressed
too far, the supernatural antagonist is not described as Yahweh, and if the name ISRAEL and PENIEL are a guide, it was
El, a Canaanite god. Lastly the location is important, it is at
the crossing of the river, the threshold of the land of Canaan,
and in popular thought, thresholds were always dangerous
to those who crossed for the first time. All this suggests
that we have here a very ancient story which, because it
had so strong a hold on the imagination, was particularly
valuable for interpretation and re-interpretation. In its final
form in the book of Genesis, it at least points to the fact
that Jacob is entering the new land, the land of promise.

He is to receive this promise not primarily by his own astuteness, but by the gift of God. It is by the power of the Blessing in his soul that Jacob is able to prevail; yet he must exert himself to do so even against the unknown and supernatural. In so doing he acquires the name ISRAEL and enters on the new life which God has prepared for him—the ancestor of his people Israel. It is to be noted that Hosea (12.4) refers to this incident, though his emphasis on Jacob's weeping and pleading does not make quite the same point as does the Genesis story. But he does relate the story to the nation Israel's relationship with God. That seems to have been the intention of Genesis. Israel's ultimate victory will come not by the usual ways by which nations gain power, but in the power of the divine blessing.

**24.** The dramatic power of the opening clause prepares the mind for what follows; A MAN appears to be in vv. 28, 30, God (or a 'god') and in Hos. 12.4 an angel. The difference is more apparent than real. In Biblical thought the agent was so clearly identified with the sender as to be virtually identified with him in the discharge of his function; note the use of the pronouns in Gen. 44.4-10.[1] UNTIL THE BREAKING OF THE DAY the Hebrew is 'until the going up of the dawn (or more precisely the dawn God)' a phrase which retains in popular idiom the belief that day came when the sun arose from his tent to course over the sky (cf. Ps. 19.4-6; Eccl. 1.5). It is a common belief that supernatural visitants have power only at night (cf. v. 26).

**25.** The supernatural being could not prevail by normal strength, so he dislocated Jacob's thigh by superhuman power.

**26.** Even so Jacob refused to let his antagonist go, and the

[1] For a careful discussion of this usage, cf. A. R. Johnson, *The One and the Many in the Israelite Conception of God*, Cardiff, 1942.

latter appears to plead for release! But Jacob, made aware
of the divine nature of his antagonist, demands a blessing,
i.e. he seeks for himself the superhuman power of his ad-
versary. This is given (vv. 27 f.) by the changing of Jacob's
name to Israel. On the one hand this is an assertion of
authority over Jacob; on the other hand the giving of a new
name meant the giving of a new life or status (cf. II Kings
23.34; 24.17). The name was a real part of the person, the
expression of his personality (cf. Deut. 12.11). ISRAEL does
not mean AS A PRINCE HAST THOU POWER (or 'persevered')
WITH GOD (or gods) AND WITH MEN; it serves however to
evoke the memory of this story. The meaning of the name
is not certain, God fights or rules, but God is the subject of
the verb. The reference to men in this verse seems out of
place. But this is part of the theological interpretation. The
story serves as an acted parable of the life of Israel, the
people of God, strong in the power of the blessing. The
word for God in Hebrew has no article and could be translated 'gods' as in Ex. 20.3 and Judg. 9.9 (gods and men).
The phrase could, alternatively, be an idiom for 'everything' (It is a strange fact that another account of the giving
of the name appears at 35.9-12 (P). The fact that that is
separated from this story suggests (a) that this story had
'proved itself' to be divine teaching in the life of Israel
in pre-exilic days and could not be discarded; but (b) it did
not lend itself to the more formal post-exilic theological
point of view.)

**29.** The divine name cannot be had on demand (cf. Judg.
13.7 f.); i.e. man cannot exercise power over God (magic);
he can only receive power from God (religion).

### 30 f. Peniel
or PENUEL (Face of El) is related to the incident. This
is an earlier interpretation of peculiar importance to a cult
centre with that name.

**32.** It is apparently another interpretation, early but more distinctively Israelite, relating the event to a food taboo.

Thus a very ancient story connected with the cult centre PENUEL (v. 30) was related to Israel's religious life (v. 32) and became the vehicle of theological teaching of the highest importance: Israel is the people in whom the divine blessing is present and by that (and that alone) can Israel prevail over the threats to her life.

## JACOB MEETS ESAU

### 33.1-16

There is a feeling of inevitability about this incident that derives from the preceding story. The successful reconciliation depends, of course, on the generosity of Esau, whose murderous resentment (27.41) has disappeared. But at a deeper level we are made to feel that the events are firmly under divine control and this is subtly suggested by v. 10b with the reference to the FACE (*pānîm*). It is still Jacob: no magical change is suggested. Yet we can perhaps detect a growing humility and confidence in God.

**1 f.** On seeing Esau with his considerable body of men, Jacob divided the family so as to put his favourite wife and her son in the position of least danger.

**3.** The seven-fold prostration is an action appropriate for a vassal to the great king. It is so described in the Tell el Amarna letters as the obeisance of a city prince to the Pharaoh. It is a formal act of homage (so also v. 8).

**4. Esau**

responds with superb generosity. The kiss is not only an emotional response; it was an act of reconciliation in which the souls of the two men were united.

**9-11.** This is the normal Oriental courtesy whereby the one at first refuses then at the insistence of the other finally accepts the gift. But to accept the gift was to accept the giver.

**12-16.** Esau's offer of protection for the journey may well have been sincere. To travel through such a territory was to be in considerable danger from marauding bands. But Jacob cannot accept it at face value; he does not place himself so completely under Esau's control. 'Protection' then as now could have a sinister meaning. In fact Jacob did not follow Esau to Edomite territory (v. 16), but after remaining for a time in Gilead (v. 17), he entered Canaan (v. 18).

## SETTLEMENT AT SHECHEM

### 33.17-20

This brief note is to prepare the mind for the story that follows (Ch. 34). But it includes an important statement, that Jacob bought some land in the district of SHECHEM. Thus Israel had ancient rights of property in both South (ch. 23) and the centre of Canaan. From another point of view, the promise to Abram (12.6) is coming nearer to fulfilment. But behind this brief note, as will appear in ch. 34, there lies a tradition of settlement which appears in the Tell el Amarna letter of about 1375 BC. This book of Genesis gives tantalizing glimpses of this period; but we have to remember that it is not primarily a history but a teaching book. Nevertheless it gives occasional glimpses of a historical situation such as we see more fully documented in extra-Biblical material.

## 17. Succoth

The name is connected with the Feast of Booths (*sukkoth*), later to become the supreme festival in Israel. It is referred to in Josh. 13.27 and Ps. 60.6, but apparently had little importance in the later history of Israel, perhaps because it was in this disputed territory of Gilead.

## 18. Shalem

should probably not be regarded as a place name though this is grammatically possible, but as a noun meaning ' in safety ' (cf. RV and RSV).

# THE CONQUEST OF SHECHEM

## Ch. 34

This chapter appears to be a presentation of a tribal event through the medium of a story concerning individuals. This is a mode of presentation which is unfamiliar to the modern Western mind, but normal to the mind of ancient Israel (cf. Hos. 11.1-4). It is obviously connected with 49.5-7.

It appears that an Israelite tribe (DINAH) was settled in the Canaanite district of Shechem and absorbed into the Canaanite community, or perhaps conquered and so lost its tribal identity Two other tribes, Simeon and Levi, although in a covenant relationship with the Shechemites, treacherously attacked them, gained a temporary advantage and sacked the city. But their action so aroused the resentment of the neighbouring Canaanites that they, in turn, suffered a decisive defeat and their tribal power was shattered. Although they fell back on territory which they had previously occupied in the neighbourhood of the Judaean clans, they were so weakened that they were unable to maintain themselves and were absorbed either into Judah (SIMEON) or into the larger tribal confederation of Israel. The situation thus presented fits well the picture presented in the Tell el Amarna letters (early fourteenth century BC), in which kings of the various city states under Egyptian suzerainty describe the incursions of the Hapiru. The district of SHECHEM in particular appears for a time to have made common cause with the invaders.

But the purpose of this story in the Book of Genesis is not merely to report an incident of Israel's ancient past. First it is pointing to the perils consequent upon the adoption of the Canaanite way of life, and the impropriety of subordinating Israelite to Canaanite culture. But it is also concerned to condemn the kind of deceit and violence which all too often characterized the settlement of nomadic tribes in Canaan. It is the will of God that Israel should retain its integrity; but this must be in God's ways and not through arrogance and violence that disregards moral considerations. In view of the fact that the rite of circumcision (cf. ch. 17) plays a prominent part in the story but with no religious significance, a protest may be indicated against an irreligious use of a sacramental rite. Circumcision is not a sign of national superiority; it is a sign of divine grace in the Covenant.

It would appear that this story existed in two forms, J and P, before it was combined into our present narrative. Both preserved the tradition that the district of SHECHEM was invaded from the South by SIMEON and LEVI; but one (P) indicates that other Israelite tribes had some share in the events (vv. 27-29). The tradition in its earlier form (J) suggests that the two tribes were acting independently of the rest and that their action was not approved (vv. 26, 30 f.). The latter view is indicated also in 49.5-7. Another tradition celebrating Israel's conquest of Shechem appears in 48.22 q.v.

**1.** Clearly the events of this chapter were thought of as taking place some considerable time after those of ch. 33, where the family of JACOB were still children, and DINAH in particular was about seven years old (cf. 31.41). But this simply emphasizes the fact that Genesis is not constructed as a history book.

## 2. Shechem

is normally the name of a city. In Judg. 9 we find the Shechemites and Israelites are living together under a king of mixed stock. HAMOR also appears in Judg. 9.28. HIVITE (cf. 10.17), a name of frequent occurrence in the Bible for one of the elements in the pre-Israelite population, but not otherwise known. DEFILED (RV, RSV, 'humbled', cf. Deut. 21.14; 22.24, 29) is a legal term and relates to the bride price which her father might otherwise obtain for her in marriage.

**3 f.** Shechem, however, wishes for marriage and, as normally, asks his father to negotiate. SOUL, the seat of emotions. SPAKE KINDLY, lit. 'spoke upon the heart' (cf. 50.21; Isa. 40.2).

## 7. wrought folly

The Hebrew word is a strong term for shameless, outrageous behaviour especially associated with irregular sexual behaviour (Deut. 22.21; Josh. 7.15; Judg. 19.23; 20.6, 10; II Sam. 13.12; Jer. 29.23), and therefore affecting the whole life of the religious community; so also the last phrase in the verse. The description of this FOLLY in Isa. 32.6 (AV, 'villany') indicates the horror aroused by this word. Yet IN ISRAEL makes it clear that the whole people, not the individuals, is referred to. Certain currently accepted standards in the ancient world were intolerable in the life of Israel.

**9 f.** A treaty of alliance is being proposed between two

H

groups of people, in which Israelites shall have equal rights with the people of this city state in matters of property and trade; in fact they shall become one people.

**13-19.** There is no suggestion here of circumcision as a sacramental rite. It is a mark of a covenant relationship, but between two sets of people whereby they become one people. Apparently also its earlier association with puberty rites is present in this story; it is a pre-requisite of marriage.

**13. deceitfully**

Perhaps 'treacherously' gives the sense of the Hebrew word. This condemnation of Israelite behaviour by an Israelite is a notable feature of the story.

**24. all that went out of the gate of the city**

(cf. 23.10). The free men of the city who had the right to make decisions affecting the city-state.

**25. boldly**

More correctly describes the state of the city feeling itself to be *secure* because of the treaty (RV, RSV, 'unawares').

**27-29.** Clearly describes a marauding raid upon a city taken by surprise.

**30.** Jacob's part in this story seems curiously ineffective, although the judgment he utters is stronger than might appear in English. The conduct of these two tribes has brought the nomadic Israelites into very grave danger, not because they have, very properly, redressed a wrong, but because of their treachery. The judgment of 49.5-7 is more vigorous.

## JACOB'S RETURN TO BETHEL AND HEBRON

### Ch. 35

Again we have a complex of ancient traditions (vv. 1-8, Northern; vv. 16-22, Southern) with later additions derived from the Priestly tradition (especially vv. 9-13, 23-29). It is not easy to relate vv. 1-15 to the account in 28.10-21 (again composite). The confusion may well have been caused by the welding together of these ancient traditions with consequent repetition (the giving of the names ISRAEL (v. 10) and BETH-EL (v. 15)). But the purpose of the story here is clear. The Jacob who received the revelation at BETH-EL as a fugitive returns now in fulfilment of his vow. Now he is to receive the full blessing, and the promise of the land for his descendants. Vv. 1-8 appear to have as their background a regular cultic practice in the Northern Kingdom, a religious pilgrimage from Shechem to Beth-el. This required the removal from the household of everything related to pagan practices, certain rites of purification, including the changing of one's clothing, and the offering of a sacrifice. It has all the appearance of a Covenant Renewal ceremony, and the additional note (vv. 9-15) is in complete accord with such an occasion. It is reasonable to suppose that the narrative has been derived from a recital made at the Beth-el shrine and so presented. To this further notes have been added to complete the story of the Patriarch, since after this chapter Jacob virtually retires from the scene and, in the main, interest centres on Joseph. It is a mark of the true-to-life quality of the Genesis material that this summary conclusion of the Jacob saga does not end in a blaze of glory. The curiously brief notes at vv. 8, 18 f., 22 seem to have been deliberately brought together. Perhaps the intention is to make impossible any kind of an-

cestor worship and to direct the mind of Israel to him alone
who can give and fulfil the blessing.

**2-4.** Describes acted renunciation of everything associated
with the worship of STRANGE (i.e. foreign to Israel) gods,
presumably in the story elements associated with Aramaean
religion (? including the *teraphim*). Ear-rings were not
merely for adornment but had a religious significance.

### 5. the terror of God
Compare the word Panic, etymologically connected with
the god Pan. The noun is used only here, but the verb is
more frequent and indicates something more powerful and
inexplicable than ordinary fear. The context relates this to
the incident in the previous chapters; but it has a more
general significance. The solemn procession, sanctified to
approach the shrine, fills the beholders with awe.

### 6. Luz . . . Beth-el
(cf. 28.19); but the form of this sentence would be natural
only if this were the first reference to LUZ. That may well
be the case in this tradition (E) while that in 28.19 is J.

**7.** EVV has smoothed out considerable difficulties in the
Hebrew. The place is never otherwise called EL-BETHEL and
cf. 31.13; the clause that follows has a plural verb, and
should be translated, ' for there the gods revealed themselves
to him . . .' This argues for the great antiquity of the story,
or the recital associated with this cult centre; it may well
be pre-Mosaic. ' The gods ' will be equivalent to the angels
of 28.12, i.e. the heavenly council.

**8.** This is the only reference to the name of REBEKAH'S
NURSE, and no explanation is offered for her presence here.
Clearly this is an isolated fragment of some tradition con-
nected with a sacred tree. A similar tradition appears in
Judg. 4.5 connected with the prophetess of the same name.

**9-13.** May be regarded as the Priestly theological interpretation of the divine revelation to Jacob, and a re-
affirmation of the blessing and the promise. When this is
read against the background of the Exile, the quality of
Israel's faith and hope becomes clear.

**15.** The naming of the sanctuary in the Priestly tradition,
as distinct from J and E.

**16-20.** The birth of BENJAMIN and death of RACHEL, the fulfilment of the hope in 30.24. The name BEN-ONI (son of my
sorrow) would be a name of ill-omen, and it was changed
to BEN-JAMIN—the right hand being the place of honour;
*jamin* also means 'south', and the tribe was the southern
part of the kingdom of Israel. But as a tribe, this people
is also known as a war-like people (cf. 49.27; Judg. 20.14-16)
troubling the Kingdom of Mari in the eighteenth century
BC.

**22.** Appears to be an attempt on the part of the eldest
son to usurp the authority of the father (cf. II Sam. 16.21 f.).
No further comment is made at this point but it is referred
to at 49.4. It is included here to account for the fact that
the rights of the elder son pass to JUDAH, the fourth of
LEAH'S sons.

**23-29.** A characteristic Priestly list. In fact Benjamin was
not born in PADAN-ARAM but in Canaan (vv. 17 f.). There
follows a statement about the death of Isaac in the presence
of Jacob. This too is hardly likely in view of what is
obviously a death-bed scene in ch. 27 (esp. 27.41). But
traditions of the ancient world do not conform to our
modern requirements. It is in fact a repetition of the scene
at the death of Abraham (25.9), a symbolical way of saying
that Isaac also was a man in whom the blessing was present.

## ESAU'S DESCENDANTS (cf. I Chron. 1.35-54)

## Ch. 36

In ch. 23.12-18 a list of the descendants of Ishmael,
Abraham's 'other' son, was given after the account of
Abraham's death. In similar fashion we are given a list, or
rather a series of lists, of Esau's family. This is considerably more extensive as might be expected in view of the
closer relationship of Israel and Edom. In view of the political relationship between Israel and Edom, as we find it
presented in the Book of Kings, it is reasonable to suppose
that this list comes from archives kept at Jerusalem. Thus,
whatever be the ultimate source of this material, its pre-
servation in this form must be due to the 'Priestly' writer;
i.e. it comes to us from the priests who took their records
with them into Exile.

The chapter contains six lists with occasional brief notes:
vv. 1-8, Esau's wives and sons; vv. 9-14, Esau's descendants; vv. 15-19, Chiefs of Edomite clans; vv. 20-30, Horite
clans and their chiefs; vv. 31-39, the Kings of Edom; vv.
40-43, Governors of Edom.

There are irreconcilable differences between vv. 1-8 and
the similar notices in 26.34; 28.9; and between vv. 1-8 and
9-14; and there appears to be some kind of connection
between vv. 9-14 and 40-43. The discrepancies make it
clear that there is nothing fictitious about these lists. They
have been faithfully copied in spite of the differences in
dealing with the same material; and they must have been
copied long after the days in which first-hand knowledge
was available. This chapter contains material of great historical importance for a knowledge of Edomite history.
But unfortunately we no longer have the key to interpret
it until some archaeological find relating to that history
should be made. By a strange irony the only information

we have about Edom in the latter part of the second millennium BC has been preserved in Israel's records. The lists
in vv. 31-39; 40-43 take us into the period of Israel's history
under the monarchy *c.* 1000 BC. That would appear to be
the reason for compiling these lists. When, under David,
Edom became part of the Israelite empire, it was obviously
important to have records of this kind.

But why should such material be preserved as part of
Israel's sacred Law? We may find the answer from observ-
ing the part played by Edom throughout the Old Testament. The chieftains of Edom are referred to in the great
recital of Ex. 15.1-18 (probably in origin a Passover recital).
Edom played a significant part in the great salvation acts
as Israel approached the land of promise (cf. Num. 20).
It is referred to in the shrine liturgies (cf. Ps. 60.8 f.; 108.9
f.). In the prophets there are numerous references to Edom,
and especially in Jeremiah (see ch. 49) and Ezekiel (ch. 25).
The noblest product of the Wisdom school was based on an
Edomite story; the scene of Job is in Edom (cf. Job 1.1;
2.11). The prophet may declare God has loved Jacob and
hated Edom (Mal. 1.1), but at least he was not indifferent
to the Edomites. It may well be that the chapter is presenting the inescapable challenge involved in the assurance that
God had chosen Israel to be the medium of revelation.
What are the implications of this for other peoples, and
especially for a neighbouring people whose fortunes were
so closely bound up with Israel? Perhaps the full answer
can only be found in the New Testament (cf. Rom. 9) where
Mal. 1.2 f. is associated with Hos. 2.23.

## 2. Hittite

(cf. 26.34). HIVITE: apparently a scribal error for HORITE
(cf. v. 20); the Hebrew words could easily be confused
*Hvy—Hry.* During recent years much has been learned
about the Horites; earlier commentaries understood the
word as meaning cave-dwellers, Heb. *hor* (Hurrians). They

were a powerful people, who broke into northern Mesopotamia from Armenia during the sixteenth and fifteenth
centuries BC and founded the important city state Nuzi.
Apparently they penetrated to Canaan and Edom, and left
the imprint of their culture upon the peoples of these lands.
AHOLIBAMAH, render 'Oholibamah' (and in v. 25).

**7.** cf. 13.6 f.

**11. Teman**
   An important district in Edom (cf. Jer. 49.7; Amos 1.12).
KENAZ, a tribe to the south of Canaan, later absorbed into
Judah (cf. 15.19; Josh. 14.6, 14; 10-14). It is to be noted
that Edom also developed a twelve tribe confederacy.

**15. Dukes**
   i.e. leaders of clans, chieftains.

**20. Horite**
   (cf. v. 2). Apparently the Hurrians formed a powerful
element in Edom.

**24. mules**
   RV and RSV 'hot springs'. The translations are uncertain; the word only appears here and no obvious cognate
has been found.

**31-39.** Edom was settled and became a state at a date considerably earlier than the Israelite settlement in Canaan (cf.
Num. 20.14). The kings were, apparently, not hereditary
but elected. It is reasonable to suppose that this list brings
the date down to David's reign, when Edom was conquered
and became a province of Israel. The period indicated
would be about 200 to 250 years, but a precise figure is
hardly possible.

**40-43.** Indicate sub-divisions of Edom and may well be
the governors appointed by David.

## C. JOSEPH (chs. 37-50)

With two interruptions (chs. 38 and 49), the rest of the book of Genesis is concerned with Joseph; all other characters are subsidiary to him. It is a sustained narrative, and continuous in a way that the account of Abraham, Isaac and Jacob are not. It is presented with a high degree of artistic skill and shows a fine understanding of character and the inner motives that govern action. Although the story begins in Canaan, most of it takes place in Egypt. The living background is therefore quite different from the preceding chapters. There is no interest in cult-centres; no account of tribal movements or relationships (this only appears in chs. 38 and 49). The characters in the story, and especially that of Joseph, are fully rounded and develop naturally. It is, in fact, literature in the best sense of the word. Ethical considerations are obviously important to the narrator, and the standard of judgment is of a high quality, yet there is no attempt to present even Joseph as an ideal figure; he is a real person. The point of view finds close parallels with the Wisdom literature of Israel and the presentation of the Joseph story, whatever be its ultimate origin, must have come from those quarters from which the Wisdom literature arose (cf. Prov. 22.29). He is the Sage whose wisdom and conduct find their motive force in the fear of the Lord. He can interpret dreams, retain his integrity in both adversity and prosperity, promote the welfare of his brethren. He knows that God is at work in all things for good; therefore he too must do what is good, even for his brothers who despitefully used him.

Yet this is not merely a story to inculcate moral precepts. It is to be read in the light of the preceding chapters and in the light of the events described in Exodus. This is made clear in Gen. 48 and in Ex. 1.6-8. Thus, while the signifi-

cance of the Joseph story in its own right, as told by the
Wisdom writer, appears in 45.7 f.; 50.20, its place in the
whole book, as part of the Torah, is made clear in ch. 48.
The blessing of Abraham is once more handed on. But this
takes place in Egypt, so that it would seem further than
ever from possible fulfilment. Yet the promise of fulfilment
is given with complete assurance (48.21; 50.24). We can
then appreciate the point of this great story for those who
were exiled from the Holy Land. The Babylonian Exile
was the death knell of all national ambition; it was also the
situation in which the real nature of Israel's faith and hope
became known. It is possible that the Joseph story was
shaped by the wise men of Israel in the days of Solomon,
when for the first time Israel began to share in the culture
and wisdom of the ancient world. But it received a new
depth of meaning in the death and rebirth of the Exile,
when it became part of Israel's Law.

It will be seen in the commentary that the material in
the Joseph story had an earlier literary and oral form. We
can clearly recognize the work of the Priestly writer in
46.6-27, and in a few brief notes elsewhere. We can recognize the welding together of traditions in the other chapters, and this recognition helps to explain the presence of
formal inconsistencies, especially in ch. 37. But the presentation of the story by, as we suppose, the sages of the
Solomonic period makes it difficult to be sure of the sources
from which they gained their material.

The plans of these chapters may be suggested as follows:

| | |
|---|---|
| 37. | How Joseph came to Egypt |
| (38. | Judah and Tamar) |
| 39-41 | Joseph's rise to eminence |
| 42-45 | Joseph and his brothers |
| 46-48 | Israel's coming to Egypt |
| (49. | The Blessing of Jacob) |
| 50. | The last acts of Joseph. |

## How Joseph Came to Egypt

### Ch. 37

**1 f.** The story opens with a characteristic Priestly formula.
It represents the story of Joseph as part of Jacob's story.
This is typical of Hebrew psychology, for while Jacob is
alive, all that happens to his family is part of his life.
Joseph's age is given as seventeen, yet strangely there is
no mention of Benjamin. The reference to the EVIL REPORT
(perhaps some dishonesty in connection with the flocks)
prepares our mind for the ill feeling.

**3.** The story of Joseph's birth in 30.22-24 is hardly com-
patible with the statement that he was the son of Jacob's
old age. This must come from a different tradition. COAT
OF MANY COLOURS or ' long-sleeved coat ' (cf. II Sam. 13.18);
the exact translation is uncertain but it was a garment fit
for a king.

**5-11.** The two dreams. It is noteworthy that the dreams
in this story always come in pairs, the second reinforcing
the first. Then dreams were understood to be a divine communication and to have a prophetic quality; i.e. they had
the power of their own fulfilment. So his family might
resent what would appear to be Joseph's youthful pride,
but they were unable to dismiss the dreams as fanciful.

### 10. thy mother
clearly supposes that Rachel is alive; evidently this
comes from a tradition independent of that in 35.19 (cf. v.
3). The following section, vv. 12-36 (with 39.1-6), shows
clear evidence of conflation. Obviously he could not be
sold both to Midianites and to Ishmaelites; nor sold to
Potiphar both by Midianites and Ishmaelites. Evidently

this story about Joseph was well-known and repeated in different circles with minor variations. This, together with the remarkably circumstantial details in the story, is evidence for its great antiquity. One tradition presents Judah as taking the lead, dissuading the rest from murder and selling Joseph to a passing Ishmaelite caravan who in turn sold him to Potiphar (vv. 12-18, 21, 25b-27, 28b, 31-35; 40.1 ff.). The other tradition had Reuben taking the lead, dissuading from bloodshed, and Midianite traders, while the brothers have their meal, take Joseph from the pit and sell him to Potiphar (vv. 19 f., 22-25a, 28a, c, 29, 36).

**12. Shechem**
is some 50 miles from Hebron, while DOTHAN (v. 17) is 13 miles further north.

**19. dreamer**
The English word hardly conveys the Hebrew expression 'master of dreams', i.e. one who has the power to receive (divinely inspired) dreams.

**21. Reuben**
has probably replaced an original Judah (cf. v. 26).

**22. shed no blood**
This was important, for shed blood 'cries out' to God (4.10). If Joseph should die in the pit this danger would be averted. The PIT was an underground rain water catchment, narrow at the top and sloping away to a broad base. It would be quite impossible to escape.

**25.** Dothan was on the caravan route from GILEAD to EGYPT. SPICERY, gum tragacanth; BALM AND MYRRH are resinous products much prized for burning as incense and for embalming.

**28. twenty pieces of silver**
(cf. Lev. 27.5 f.) the recognized value for a young slave.

**29.** REUBEN as the eldest brother was chiefly responsible.

**35.** Jacob will wear mourning until he dies; characteristic hyperbole for inconsolable grief. GRAVE, Heb.
*Sheol* the place of the lingering shade after death, where
all living distinctions were obliterated in barely conscious
existence (cf. Ps. 6.5). The OT has no doctrine of im-
mortality and the hope of Resurrection did not arise until
a very late date (cf. Dan. 12.2). One of the distinctive
features of the OT is its freedom from crass ideas about
life after death and the eventual hope based entirely on a
living relationship with God.

**36. Potiphar**
An Egyptian name meaning 'He whom the god Ra
gives'. OFFICER, literally 'eunuch', but the word was commonly used for an official of the court. Similarly the word
for 'bodyguard' originally meant 'butcher' (cf. I Sam.
9.23, 'cook'); so also in 39.1; 40.3 f.; 41.10, 12.

JUDAH AND TAMAR

## Ch. 38

The interest of this chapter is in tribal history—presented under the normal convention of a story about individuals. It indicates the manner in which the tribe of
Judah established itself in the South by making alliance
with Canaanite elements, how for a time it was in danger
of disappearing but was able through further Canaanite
alliance to establish itself and so give rise to the important
clans of Perez and Zerah.

What is difficult to understand is why this should be presented in so scandalous a form. The only person in the
story who emerges with credit is the Canaanite woman
TAMAR. Her conduct may seem questionable to the modern
mind, but in the situation described she was fulfilling the
all-important duty of providing a family for her husband.
It is to be understood in the light of Deut. 25.5-10, the law of
levirate marriage, a custom widely accepted in the ancient
world, though the extreme form in Gen. 38 would not have
commended itself to later Israel. Perhaps the ancient tradition was presented in this form as a vigorously expressed
parable. Thus the divine purpose for the continuance of
Judah was fulfilled in spite of the folly and ill-conduct of
those through whom it was to be fulfilled. This does not
excuse Judah, but it does underline the sovereignty of divine
grace at work in those who are least worthy of it. It will be
recalled that Tamar (like Rahab the harlot and Ruth the
Moabite) is specifically referred to in the genealogy of the
Messiah in Matt. 1.3, 5.

It is also difficult to understand the inclusion of this
story in its present position, for it harshly interrupts the
sequence between 37.36 and 39.1. It is appropriate that
something should be said of Judah, since after the settlement the Judahite tribe shares in importance with the
Josephite tribes, Ephraim and Mannasseh, and ultimately
emerged as the people in whom 'Israel' was continued. In
spite therefore of its harsh interruption, its place is not inappropriate when (apparently) Joseph is lost to Israel.

**1.** Judah's independence of his brothers is reflected in the
later history (cf. Judg. 1.1-20). The tribe is not summoned
in the Song of Deborah to take a place in the confederacy.
Adullam was about 10 miles N.W. of Hebron.

**2.** The marriage to a Canaanite woman occasions no condemnation in this chapter in contrast to 28.6 (P).

## 3. Er
(I Chron. 4.21) is a son of Shelah, i.e. a subdivision of the clan. Apparently the Er clan was once strong and later declined in power.

## 4. Onan
cf. I Chron. 2.26.

## 5. Shelah
cf. Num. 26.20; I Chron. 4.21. CHEZIB apparently the same as Achzib (Josh. 15.44).

**7.** No explanation of Er's wickedness is given. It may be an inference from his death at an early age.

## 8. marry
The Hebrew here is a technical term meaning ' perform the duty of a brother-in-law to raise a family for the dead man ', i.e. levirate marriage. The custom was widespread in the ancient world and is known in Assyrian, Hittite and Hurrian law as well as in Israel (Deut. 25. 5-10). Only two occurrences are referred to in the OT, here and Ruth, neither of which corresponds exactly to the law. It may be assumed that what is described here was modified in the later Israelite law.

**10.** Having refused to fulfil his sacred obligation, he was slain by Yahweh.

## 11. Judah
feared that TAMAR was responsible (cf. Tobit 3.8), and dishonestly delayed action. But to return Tamar to her father's household was, in effect, to repudiate her. This, by contemporary standards, would justify her in her subsequent course of action. She was resolved to continue the family of her dead husband. The means she adopted were

in no way offensive in Oriental religion. In fact the word
for HARLOT used here is a technical term meaning 'holy
woman'. (Such practices were repudiated in later Israelite
law and condemned by the prophets, cf. Deut. 23.17.) She
was performing a proper, indeed religious, action. She then
claimed as a pledge that the correct compensation be paid,
the seal bearing Judah's name, and the staff which was the
sign of his status as a chieftain. The climax comes in vv.
24-26. Judah was quick to assume his responsibility to condemn the woman who was technically betrothed to his son!
But in fact he was compelled to recognize his own failure
to fulfil the law, since he had not married her to Shelah.

**26.** She was in the right in this matter.

The closing verses repeat in somewhat different form the
story of the birth of Esau and Jacob (25.24-26). The truly
elder brother becomes subordinate to the younger, a clear
reflection of clan rivalry in which the Perez clan gained
supremacy (cf. I Chron. 2.5 ff.). PHAREZ suggests the word
for breaking out; ZARAH suggests bright scarlet, although
a different word is used in verse 28.

One striking feature of this story is the decisive role
played by a woman. She is the only one who receives praise
in this narrative. We are made to feel that the future of the
tribe of Judah depended on her. This recognition of the
decisive importance of the woman is not unique in the Old
Testament (cf. Deborah, Ruth, Esther). But it is a remarkable fact that a strongly masculine society should give such
prominence to these stories.

## JOSEPH'S RISE TO EMINENCE

### Chs. 39-41

The Joseph story is now resumed from 37.36. The slave

rose to a position of responsibility in his master's household, but was unjustly imprisoned. This however was to be the opportunity through which he rose to a position of greatest eminence under the Pharaoh. This might well have been presented as a reward appropriate to a virtuous man. In fact it is not so presented. The specific occasion in which Joseph's virtue is demonstrated resulted in his being thrown into prison! The point is made with great artistry that both in ill fortune and good, God was with him (39.2, 3, 21), that his success was due to divine action (39.2, 3, 21, 23), that his virtue (39.9), his skill (40.8; 41.16, 25, 38) and his prosperity (41.52) were God's work. Joseph was no self-made man; this is not, in the ordinary sense of the word, a success story. It is an exposition of the wisdom that is begotten of 'the fear of the Lord', i.e. true religion. Wisdom, for Israel, was more than intellectual knowledge; it meant that grasp of reality which enabled a man rightly to discern the issues of life and rightly to conduct his life by that insight. If, then, we are right in seeing this story, in its present form, as deriving from the sages of Solomon's court and shaped by them to serve the interests of Yahweh religion (whatever be the earlier history of various elements in the story), we have an understanding of Israel's early Wisdom teaching and the work of inspiration in that medium.

**39.** The first act in the drama shows us Joseph, a slave rising to a position of trust, resisting temptation, and unjustly thrown into prison.

**1.** cf. 37.36. Nowhere in the Joseph story is the Pharaoh identified, and any attempt more exactly to define even the dynasty must be regarded as speculative. An identification that would well suit the story (with the sequel in Ex. 1.8) would be Ikhnaton, c. 1370 BC, though many would relate the story to the Hyksos period, seventeenth century BC. Pharaoh is a title meaning literally 'the great house'.

**2. prosperous**

Better 'successful'.

**4. Joseph**

attracted favourable attention, and becomes first a personal attendant, then superintendent of the household.

**6.** Joseph was 'handsome and good looking' (RSV). This leads to the events of vv. 7-20. This story is a close parallel to an ancient Egyptian story of two brothers, the younger of whom similarly repulses the wife of the elder and is falsely accused of attempted rape. Joseph's conduct illustrates the wisdom teaching of Prov. 2.10-22; 7.6-27.

**9.** Render with RSV 'he is not greater in this house than I am'. But the evil is not only morally wrong; it is sin (literally 'missing the mark') against God (cf. Ex. 20.14, etc.).

**14. Hebrew**

A term rarely used in the OT, but five times in the Joseph story and usually by an Egyptian in a derogatory sense, 'a foreign slave'. MOCK: the same word as in 26.8.

**20.** Adultery, even by a free citizen, was punishable by death. Why Joseph was merely imprisoned remains unexplained. It has been suggested that Potiphar was not entirely convinced about his wife's story; but that seems unlikely. If an explanation is needed it must be seen in the repeated statement THE LORD WAS WITH JOSEPH. In fact his imprisonment is merely the necessary prelude to the next act of the drama of which vv. 21-23 set the scene.

**21. shewed him mercy**

Literally 'stretched unto him his steadfast love'. Egyptian prisons are no hindrance to Yahweh!

## THE DREAMS OF THE TWO EGYPTIAN
## OFFICIALS

### Ch. 40

As in the stories about Daniel, so here Joseph is skilled in the interpretation of dreams, but his skill is attributed by him to divine activity. The butler and the baker were high officials at the Egyptian court. What their offence was is not told; it is rather suggested that they were merely victims of the Pharaoh's arbitrary anger. They remained in custody for some time (v. 4), awaiting trial. THE CAPTAIN OF THE GUARD is exactly the same phrase as is used of Potiphar (37.36; 39.1), and he CHARGED JOSEPH as though he were still his slave, in some contrast to 39.23. Chs. 39 and 40 were originally independent stories.

5. Dreams were believed to contain, usually in a concealed fashion, a prediction of future events, and normally needed a skilled interpreter. So far as we can determine from the OT, Israelite faith was remarkably free from the puerilities of dream interpretation found in contemporary culture. The reason is given in v. 8: God, that is the holy and gracious God whom Israel came to know, and he alone, can give the interpretation. Dream interpretation, Israel would say, is not an exact science under man's control. It is a product of trust in and loyalty to God. This, in the contemporary situation, is a much more important belief than a dismissal of dreams as meaningless. Indeed Joseph's statement might be regarded as a challenge to the diviners of the ancient world. The dreams as recounted in vv. 9-19 are appropriate to the functions of the officials. The first dream is favourable. To lift up his head (v. 13) is a mark of favour. The interpretation of the second dream should be said aloud, with a pause after HEAD (v. 19). It is a terrible

play on words (perhaps an oblique reference to most of the ambiguous oracles that have been preserved from extra-Israelite sources), and points to another kind of lifting up, by hanging.

**15. land of the Hebrews**
An obvious indication of a later period. At this time it was the land of Canaan.

**16. three white baskets**
Better 'three baskets of white bread'.

**17. bakemeats**
i.e. baked food or pastry (cf. margin and RSV).

**23.** cf. Eccl. 9.15.


JOSEPH AT PHARAOH'S COURT

## Ch. 41

This is the final act in this part of the drama, though the climax is but the beginning of a drama produced by it. It describes that series of events in which, so obviously to the reader, God is at work for the good of the one whom he has chosen and who is loyal to him.

**1. the river**
i.e. the Nile. The Hebrew word used here is derived from the Egyptian word for the Nile; so in vv. 2, 3, 17, 18.

**2-8.** The two dreams clearly had the same meaning, portended some evil, but could not be more precisely explained.

**3 f.** Render 'sleek and fat' . . . 'gaunt and thin' (RSV).

**5-7.** Render 'fat and good' . . . 'thin and scorched' (by the hot dry sirocco).

**8.** The attempt to interpret by the 'science' of dream interpretation fails (cf. Dan. 2). The frequent repetition in vv. 9-24 is a mark of good story telling whereby the hearers' fuller participation is gained.

### 9. I do remember
Would be more naturally translated 'I make mention of . . .' (so RV m.). It is a formal confession of guilt.

**14.** Shaving the beard was an Egyptian custom, but not Israelite.

**15.** '. . . when thou hearest a dream thou canst interpret'.

**16.** '. . . Not I! . . . a favourable answer'. The interpretation of the dreams (vv. 25-32) is followed by practical advice (vv. 33-36). This is a good example of what was understood by wisdom, and the point is made by Pharaoh that this superlative wisdom was the work of the spirit of God (v. 38). All unusual powers, physical (Samson's strength, Judg. 15.14), artistic (Ex. 28.3) or administrative as here, were understood as the working of this divine energy. The same word is used for 'wind' (cf. Ezek. 37.1-14).

### 40. over my house
The king's chief minister (cf. I Kings 4.6, etc.). BE RULED; the Hebrew word here is difficult, literally 'shall kiss'. It may be a scribal error for a word meaning 'pay heed' (cf. LXX). The elevation of a slave to such a post is not without parallel in other Oriental empires, and in the Roman empire.

**42. his ring**

is the signet ring, making Joseph the royal representative.

**43. Bow the knee**

This is translating an unusual form of the Hebrew verb 'to kneel'. More probably it is a Hebraized form of an Egyptian word whose meaning may be 'pay heed'.

**45-52.** *Joseph's family.* His Egyptian name means 'The god speaks and he lives'. He marries the daughter of an Egyptian high-ranking priest. Her name means 'Belonging to (the goddess) Neith'. Her father's name is that borne by Joseph's earlier master; ON, called by the Greeks Heliopolis, north of Cairo, the centre of Sun-worship. All this seems entirely alien to the point of view represented in 24.3 f., etc. This may also be due to the influence of the Wisdom school who were much more open to extra-Israelite influences.

**51 f.** The names are as usual associated with appropriate explanations: 'caused me to forget' (*naššani*); i.e. so blessed Joseph that the separation did not produce bitter repining; Ephraim is associated with CAUSED ME TO BE FRUITFUL (*hiphrani*). In fact the name is a descriptive term for a locality, Ephraim—the fruitful corn land.

**53-57.** Joseph's measures were successful beyond expectation. Enough was stored to supply the needs of Egypt and of neighbouring peoples.

**56. all the storehouses**

This is a correct emendation of an untranslatable Hebrew text, 'all that is in them'.

**57.** Prepares the way for the next act.

## JOSEPH AND HIS BROTHERS

### Chs. 42-45

## THE FIRST MEETING

### Ch. 42

Famine compels Jacob to send his sons to Egypt, but he retains Benjamin. They meet Joseph, but do not recognize him after the passage of the years (about twelve in one tradition, 41.1, 48; 45.6, or about twenty, cf. 37.3; 41.46, plus seven years of good harvests). They are at first suspected of being spies, then released (leaving Simeon in ward) to bring Benjamin back to Joseph.

There is evidence that the story has been compiled from two forms of it. Thus, v. 35, they find the money at the end of their journey for they had no need to open their sacks, since Joseph had given them enough food for man and beast for their journey (v. 25). But (vv. 27 f.) they found the money after only one day's travelling. Again, Simeon's detention (42.24) is ignored in 43.3-7. The differences are small but sufficient to indicate that the account of Joseph in Egypt was told in more than one circle before it was written down. Ch. 41; 42.1-26, 29-37; 43.14 and most of ch. 45 appear to derive from the Northern tradition, while 42.27-28, 38; 43.1-13, 15-34; and ch. 44 derive from Judah. But the traditions considerably overlapped.

The reader's mind has already been prepared for the fact that the evil conduct of the brothers has been overruled by God to work for good. That good is necessarily, but not only, to provide food; they must also recognize and be chastened for the evil they have done.

Egypt was the natural source of food in times of famine, since it was normally a great grain-producing country.

Egyptian inscriptions and carvings refer to the coming of
Asiatics in search of food. Yet in the fourteenth century
the Egyptian would naturally look with suspicion on such
bands in view of the troubles in the land of Canaan. The
reference to spies is entirely appropriate. So also is the
reluctance of Jacob to let his youngest son, the only sur-
vivor, as he supposes, of the children of Rachel, travel this
dangerous route.

**1. Why do you look one upon another**
In helpless despair.

**6. bowed down themselves**
A subtle reminder of the dream (37.7 f.).

**7. he knew them, but made himself strange**
i.e. behaved like a foreigner. The two verbs are in
Hebrew two parts of the same verb. They would naturally
not recognize the exalted Egyptian official as their younger
brother.

**13-24.** With great skill the brothers are made to remember
their evil conduct. The testing process ('proved', vv. 15,
16) may indicate Joseph's natural fear that the brothers
had treated Benjamin as they had treated him. So Simeon
(not the eldest, Reuben, who had wished to help Joseph) is
kept as surety. It may be observed that Joseph was exacting
from the brothers far less than they deserved.

**25-38.** By replacing their money, Joseph is treating them
like honoured guests. His generosity only serves to deepen
their sense of guilt and fear of an avenging God.

**38. to the grave**
*Sheol* (cf. 37.35).

## THE SECOND MEETING

## Ch. 43

The famine continued and Jacob commands them to go again to Egypt. Now it is Judah who takes the lead and tells the story of Joseph's command. Eventually Jacob agrees. On their arrival they are treated with great courtesy, but the only effect is to increase their fears. By various signs Joseph seeks to awaken their minds to the truth about himself. Benjamin receives special honour; yet still Joseph remains the Egyptian official.

**3. see my face**
i.e. be granted an audience.

**7. asked us**
i.e. 'inquired carefully about us and our kindred' COULD WE KNOW WITH CERTAINTY?

**10. this second time**
Render with margin, 'We could have returned twice by now'.

**11.** Jacob prepares to send the gifts that are appropriate to the high dignitary, as well as to return the money in proof of their honesty. BEST FRUITS an unusual use of the Hebrew word for 'strength'; perhaps more generally 'the best products' viz. fragrant gums, honey and pistachio nuts. This was the proper courtesy.

**14. God Almighty**
cf. 17.1.

**15. slay**
Slaughter an animal for the meal.

**21. in full weight**

There were no coins at this time and silver or gold was weighed.

**23.** Their anxiety is met by a gracious salutation, a dismissal of their concern about money—' your gods must have put it in your sacks! '

**32.** The Egyptians would eat separately from foreigners on ritual grounds. The places were appointed for the brothers in the correct order of seniority; a deliberate clue.

**33.** As a special mark of honour, portions of food (MESSES is an old English word for the portions of food) were sent from the host's table, and the most honourable for Benjamin. It was a sign of politeness to drink freely on such a festive occasion. This final sentence finely reduces the tension that has grown in this chapter and is to be increased in the following.

## THE FINAL TEST

## Ch. 44

The aim of this chapter is to bring to the surface the deeply hidden guilt of the brothers. They must realize what they have done, not only as it affects them, but as it affects their father; they must be willing to bear the consequences of their evil deed (v. 16). This is made clear by Judah acting as the eldest brother, and so the one on whom the burden of guilt of the brothers must fall (vv. 18 ff.). This must be accepted fully and freely, and not under the wrong kind of emotional stress such as would be unavoidable had Joseph been recognized. It is only then that the word of reconciliation (45.5, 7 f.) could be heard.

This time the brothers not only have their money returned to them (though nothing further is heard about this), but Joseph's divining cup is placed in Benjamin's sack. The cup was used (vv. 5, 15) for purposes of divination, the method being that of relating the shapes taken by small objects thrown into the cup filled with liquid. The discovery of the apparent theft exposes them to the danger of death or at least enslavement. This leads to the speech of Judah (vv. 18-34) in which the whole story is recounted, and ends with a noble plea that, he, Judah, shall be substitute for the young Benjamin. It is not a plea of innocence, or for extenuation of the guilt. It is an acceptance of the fact that an ancient evil has mysteriously (v. 16) caught up with the brothers. It is also evidence of a change of heart. The brothers do not propose to dispose of their father's favourite son (v. 20) as they had done with Joseph, even though this time they would have had a good excuse. Judah, in the name of his brothers, will take the full burden of apparent guilt.

### 29. sorrow

More correctly ' evil '. That meant that Jacob would die and go to *sheol*, bearing among the shades the misfortune of his last days. Thus he will go to the place of the dead with shame, and his name will be a name of ill-omen among the living.

## THE RECONCILIATION

### Ch. 45

This eloquent and unselfish plea of Judah provided the way for Joseph fully to disclose himself. But it is not merely the Joseph who had been grievously wronged, but one who is to be a saviour of those who had wronged him. The

family is to be reunited beyond expectation and in circumstances that none could foresee. Moreover the family is to
be removed from conditions of famine, to live as honoured
guests in a land of plenty. Appropriately enough in this
Eastern story, the events are reported to the Pharaoh and
he is moved by them to share in the rejoicing and to act
with great generosity to this reunited family. The chapter
closes with a very human scene of the aged father at first
incredulous and unable to bear the revival of his grief, but
finally restored at the prospect of seeing again the beloved
son he had supposed to be dead.

The great artistry of this story lies in the fact that the
reader knows that reconciliation will take place, yet cannot
see how it will be effected. He must share in the emotions
and reactions of all the parties concerned, and the manner
in which the story is told compels this participation. Yet
the story with its climax at this point is singularly appropriate to Israel's understanding of reality. In this is a representation in human terms of the long drama of God's
dealings with his people. It was the rejected God who could
not abandon his sinful people and effected their salvation
(cf. especially Hos. 2.14-23; 11.1-11 and also Ps. 37.23;
Prov. 16.9; 19.21). The point is made with great simplicity
and so the more profoundly in this chapter at vv. 5 and 7
(cf. 50.20). The key to the story of Joseph lies not so much
in the events that took place, not even in the fact that
Joseph was a man of integrity, but in the presence and
constant activity of God as Israel knew him.

**1.** Joseph had something to say to his brothers which concerns them only, and could in the first instance only be
understood by them.

### 3. doth my father yet live?

This would be quite inappropriate in the light of 43.26 f.;
44.24-34, but these verses come from the J tradition, and

there were evidently some variations in the E tradition.
TROUBLED, render 'dismayed'. The Hebrew verb suggests
a profound emotional disturbance.

### 7. to preserve you a posterity

Literally ' to set for you a remnant ' (cf. margin and RSV).
TO SAVE . . . GREAT DELIVERANCE, literally 'to keep alive a
great escaping' (cf. RSV). Both the words 'remnant' and
'escaping' appear in Isaiah with a new significance in the
light of the Assyrian invasion. But the thought of rescue
from apparently overwhelming disaster is frequent in Genesis as in other parts of the Old Testament and is well illus-
trated in Judg. 2.11–11.33.

### 8. father

A conventional Egyptian title for an able administrator.

### 10. Goshen

This appears to be the district round the Wadi Tumilat,
a narrow valley some thirty miles long connecting the Nile
with Lake Timsah, i.e. at the Eastern end of the Nile delta.
It was a very fertile district, but being on the borders of
the desert was also exposed to attack from raiders, or again
would be the first to feel the impact of invasion. Egyptian
records tell of wandering tribes receiving the Pharaoh's
permission to settle in this district in times of famine. NEAR
UNTO ME. This must be a relative term (cf. 46.34). They
were nearer than they would have been had they remained
in Canaan, but some distance from the Egyptian capital.

**16-20.** The Pharaoh's invitation is couched in terms characteristic of Oriental generosity, and worthy of the great
King.

**22 f.** Again it is characteristic to refer in some detail to the
gifts, princely in magnificence, that the great official sends.
The specific mention of CHANGES OF RAIMENT is typical.

**24.** The closing sentence is a fine example of the down-to-earth quality of the story. Ideally the thought of such a quarrelling might seem impossible after such an experience. In fact there could easily arise contention about who was most to blame.

**26. fainted**

Literally 'grew numb' or 'went cold'. What is meant is that he collapsed. But the concrete evidence that his sons' story was true revived him.

## ISRAEL'S COMING TO EGYPT

### Chs. 46-48

Just as the drama of ch. 39-41 prepared the way for that of chs. 42-45, so that in turn prepares the way for a narrative which will have its climax in the transmission of the divine blessing. This section is less dramatic in form than the preceding sections and in many ways approximates more in form to the blessing stories of Abraham and Jacob. Further we are much more aware in this section that it is pointing towards a fulfilment beyond the Genesis narrative, viz. the Exodus and Settlement in Canaan. It is providing the answer to the inevitable question prompted, for example, by the Passover celebration, 'How did our fathers come to be in Egypt and how were they treated there?' It is appropriate then that the material should be derived from various sources, the shrine teaching for the ordinary Israelite, and the Priestly tradition; the discontinuity is much more obvious (note the 'intrusion' of 46.6-27). Yet the presence of these different traditions is evidence of the care with which the ancient 'salvation facts' were preserved. They were preserved because they were necessary to the faith of Israel and productive of faith in new and apparently destructive situations.

The material in these chapters may be divided up as follows: —

| | |
|---|---|
| 46.1-7 | The migration |
| 46.8-27 | Jacob's descendants |
| 46.28–47.12 | Settlement in Goshen |
| 47.13-26 | Joseph's agrarian policy |
| 47.27-31 | The last days of Jacob |
| 48.1-22 | The blessing of Ephraim and Manasseh |

Within these chapters, especially in ch. 46, there are, to the Western mind, formal difficulties that are perhaps insoluble if we read this as a continuous narrative. The difficulties have been noted by the earlier Jewish commentators, but hardly explained. When, however, attention is paid to the earlier sources from which this narrative has been gathered together, the formal inconsistencies will be seen as arising from the combining of the traditions rather than from the traditions themselves. Particular difficulties will be noted at the appropriate verses, but we may distinguish here the Priestly material (46.6-27; 47.5-6a, 7-11, 27b-28; 48.3-7), from the more popular shrine teaching of the rest, though this also has been compiled from various traditions.

**46.1-7.** Jacob apparently dwelt at Hebron (37.14); as far as BEER-SHEBA he was still in the land of promise. Before he will leave, he must seek guidance from the God who had manifested himself at Beer-sheba to his father (26.24 f.). The point is made that the migration to Egypt is not in fact due to human interests but to a divine command. In view of the subsequent Exodus story and the later condemnation of any political relationship between Israel and Egypt, this was an important element in the shrine teaching. Long before the Exodus, it was in the divine purpose that the mighty work of salvation should be wrought in that land. No hint of that tremendous event is given in this passage; but it is explicitly noted that the stay in Egypt shall be a temporary one.

**4. bring thee up**
refers not to Jacob, the individual, but to his descendants, the people of Israel. The whole community, composed of its past, present and future members was, in Hebrew thought, considered as unified in the soul of the ancestor (cf. Jer. 31.15). So a man lived on in his descendants. PUT HIS HAND. Joseph, the favourite son, would close his father's eyes at death.

**5.** describes the departure, while vv. 6 f. (P) repeats this.

**8-27.** The figures given in this list are difficult.

**26.** gives a total of 66; v. 27 a total of 70, though the addition of Joseph and his two sons would only give 69. Further, ER and ONAN had already died (v. 12) and the number 33 in v. 15 can only be obtained by including Jacob himself and Dinah. Further, BENJAMIN has consistently been described as a youth in the story, yet in v. 21 he has ten sons. Again, the time sequence of the story would hardly allow for grandsons to JUDAH and ASHER (vv. 12, 17). It may well be that the number 70 was originally intended to be a round number (cf. Ex. 24.9; Judg. 8.30), and then in our list treated as an exact number. Most of the names appear again in Num. 26.5 ff., and again in I Chron. 2-8, with some variations. Those in vv. 9-11 appear in Ex. 6.14-16; in Ex. 6.14-20 it is to be noted, Moses is represented as the great grandson (or, through his mother, grandson) of Levi, and they may give some indication of the period of time covered by the life of Israel in Egypt.

There are many indications in the Old Testament that not all the Israelite tribes were in Egypt; yet what made Israel was the great act of salvation wrought for those in

Egypt. So as various clans associated with those who, having been released from Egypt, settled in Canaan, they
shared in the saving faith in the God who brought them
'out of the house of bondage'. This passage, like much
else in this Priestly tradition, appears to present that faith
in its own characteristic form.

**46.28–47.12.** The pronoun in v. 28 clearly continues the
narrative of vv. 1-7. Judah acts as the eldest son. TO DIRECT
HIS FACE. This is hardly a translation of the Hebrew, and
the ancient versions have renderings which indicate either
a different verb ('appear' or 'meet') or an inability to
understand the Hebrew. RSV renders 'appear before him',
from the Samaritan and Syriac versions.

**31-34.** This skilful diplomatic approach to the Pharaoh
seems to ignore 45.16-20. It is designed to give them the
right to settle, but to discourage the possibility of their
being absorbed into the Egyptian population. Apparently
cattle-rearing and sheep-tending were regarded as necessary
but low-grade occupations among the Egyptians, although
there is no Egyptian evidence to support the vigorous note
at the end. It also seems to be somewhat at variance with
47.1-12. We may perhaps regard it as a later comment
added to the original story to give emphasis. It is undoubtedly true that the Egyptians would look with suspicion upon a group of Asiatic nomads after their
experience of the Hyksos invasion and conquest.

**47.5, 6.** The Hebrew text is here somewhat confused. The
beginnings of v. 5 does not follow the request of v. 4, and
the end of v. 6 reads like a clumsy repetition of the beginning. The Greek version seems to preserve the original
order of the clauses after v. 4, 'And Pharaoh said unto
Joseph, Let them dwell in the land of Goshen; and if thou
knowest any able men among them, THEN MAKE THEM

K

RULERS OVER MY CATTLE' (this is then followed by the
Priestly account): 'And Jacob and his sons came into
Egypt unto Joseph. And Pharaoh King of Egypt heard of
it. And Pharaoh spake unto Joseph, saying, 'THY FATHER
. . . DWELL'. This, continuing into vv. 7-11, is the Priestly
account of the coming into Egypt. This order is almost
certainly the original.

## 9. pilgrimage
The Hebrew word is usually translated 'sojourning' and
simply refers to Jacob's semi-nomadic life (cf. Heb. 11.13).
FEW by comparison with the ages of Abraham (175) and
Isaac (180) according to P. EVIL dogged with misfortune.

## 11. the land of Rameses
The district was so called during the time of the oppres-
sion under Rameses II (1290-1223 BC), cf. Ex. 1.11.

## 12. families
More correctly 'little ones' (cf. margin); so RSV,
'according to the number of their dependents'.

**47.13-26.** This section appears rather abruptly and makes
no reference to the immediately preceding narrative. Indeed it follows most naturally upon ch. 41, and may well
originally have belonged to that earlier story before these
ancient traditions were used in Genesis. The measures
adopted by Joseph must be understood in the light of contemporary Egyptian conditions. The Pharaoh was an absolute monarch, in fact the living embodiment of the god
to whom the whole land belonged. Part of the land was
alienated from the king's control through its appropria-
tion by the temples (cf. v. 22, a note in full accord with
what is known from Egyptian records). From time to time
vigorous nobles secured a semi-independent control of
land, and there was (as also in European history) a constant

struggle between the king and his feudal nobles. What is being described is a situation by which the king, through the skill of his chief minister, was able to seize the opportunity to regain his domination over the land. The situation described in Genesis accords well with what is known to have taken place in Egypt after the expulsion of the Hyksos kings. The contemporary estimate of Joseph's actions is indicated in v. 25. Finally, it should be noted that the 20 per cent interest charged on the loan of seed corn was very low by contemporary standards.

His measures are in three stages (1) The corn was sold for money until all the money was in the royal treasury (v. 14). (2) Then it was exchanged for livestock (vv. 15-17). Naturally the original owners were left in charge, but must give account to the treasury and the people became the Pharaoh's serfs (vv. 18-21).

**17. fed**

The Hebrew verb means 'led with care' (cf. Ex. 15.13; Isa. 40.11); i.e. Joseph carefully led them through the crisis, with food in exchange for their cattle.

**21.** We should read with the ancient versions 'he made bondmen of them from . . .' (so RSV) in accordance with v. 19. The difference in Hebrew is slight.

**47.27-31.** The account of Jacob's death is at first described in conventional terms and then expanded with the blessing story of ch. 48. The reader's attention is drawn (a) to the confident expectation of a return fo the land of promise; (b) to the transmission of the blessing to Joseph's sons and especially to the younger, Ephraim. The former is part of the expansion of Israel's ancient creed; the latter part of its salvation-history. This section begins with the formal language of the Priestly source and continues with the Southern tradition (J). The following chapter derives in the

main (except for vv. 3-7 (P)) from the Northern tradition (E).
The form of the oath in v. 29 is that of 24.2 (q.v.). The
family sepulchre is presumably that in Machpelah (ch. 23)
though in 50.5 reference is made to a sepulchre made by
Jacob. The closing sentence is difficult and appears to have
been differently understood by the Greek-speaking Jewish
translators of the LXX (third century BC). The same consonants can be translated BED (so EVV from the Hebrew
Bible) or 'staff' (so LXX and Heb. 11.21). In general the
action suggests adoration or thanksgiving, but its precise
significance is unknown.

## THE BLESSING OF EPHRAIM AND MANASSEH

### Ch. 48

Except for the Priestly insertion (vv. 3-7) this tradition
does not record a blessing to Joseph, but to his sons. This
seems to relate to the tribal history in which at an early
date the Joseph tribe ceased to exist as a unity, but appeared in two sections, EPHRAIM and MANASSEH, and that
the former superseded the latter in political importance.
That is the situation as we see it in Judg. 5.14. These tribes,
which settled in the central part of Canaan, were politically
the most important part of the Israelite confederacy until
the downfall of the Northern Kingdom in 721 BC. Thus the
'elder son's' blessing is given to them (v. 5), though they
are the sons of a younger son.

**1.** is evidently a new beginning and not continuous with
the tradition in 47.31.

**7. by me**
lit. 'upon me' i.e. as a burden upon me and so render
'to my grief' (cf. RSV). The giving of the blessing (vv.

8 ff.) ensures the prosperity according to ancient thought (cf. ch. 27).

### 9. I will bless
It is possible that the boys were placed on his knees (cf. v. 12); the verb BLESS and the noun 'knee' have the same consonants. This suggests a symbolic act of adoption (cf. 30.3; 50.23).

**12.** Render 'took them from his knees' (cf. RSV). The careful description of vv. 13 ff. is intended to draw attention to the unexpected fact that the younger receives the blessing appropriate to the elder. The right hand as the more powerful gives the more favourable blessing, because it conveyed more of the soul or life force of him who blessed.

### 14. guiding . . . wittingly
This may be correct; but it is possible to derive the word from another root which would give the meaning 'crossing' (so RSV) and this may be the origin of the ancient versions 'changing'.

### 15. Fed
Better 'led' (as a shepherd leads his flock to pasture. It is the word which appears in Ps. 23.1, 'shepherd').

### 16. redeemed
i.e. claimed for his own and acted the part of the kinsman. This is the only occurrence in Genesis of this word which was to have such great significance in later prophetic teaching (cf. Isa. 41. 14, etc.). It suggests a sacred obligation to come to the help of the member of the family who has suffered loss. MY NAME: Jacob claims them as his own sons; they are to be reckoned above all others as the true family.

**20. Israel**

Here is a reference to the nation and clearly reflects a time when the nation was in existence.

**22. one portion**

(Heb. *shekem*, shoulder) a deliberate reference to the place ' Shechem ' (shoulder, i.e. mountain slope). The reference to Jacob's conquest of Shechem clearly alludes to a tradition other than that of ch. 34, and one that is not otherwise referred to. Here Jacob takes the credit for the conquest of Shechem. This may, again, relate to the later historical situation, since Jacob in Egypt could hardly bequeath the Canaanite city.

## THE BLESSING OF JACOB

### Ch. 49

Formally this is a long poem uttered by the aged Jacob on his death-bed. It is clearly unrelated to the preceding and succeeding chapters. A careful examination suggests that it is a compilation of very diverse material, blessings, curses and statements of fact. It would be simplest to regard this as a compilation of poetical utterances preserved in or concerning the tribal groups; it should be compared with Deut. 33.6-25 and Judg. 5.14-18. The very obscurity of some of the passages suggests their great antiquity, and that in some instances their exact significance had been lost before they were included in this collection. Some uncertainty must remain about the date of the various parts of the ' Blessing '; most of the tribal references would suggest the period before the institution of the monarchy, yet the description of Judah and Joseph would be more appropriate to a period after the breaking of the Philistine yoke. Undoubtedly the material precedes Deut. 33; its relation to

Judg. 5 is less certain. The fact is that the history of the
individual tribes in Canaan before the Davidic monarchy
is too little known to permit a firm dating of this material.
It presents us with a picture of a loosely connected, twelve-
tribe (perhaps originally six, the Leah tribes, and then extended) confederacy, but not so closely related as to form
a nation.

A further point of comparison is with the tribal lists in
Num. 1 and 26, where there are variations in the order, the
omission of Levi and the consequent reckoning of Ephraim
and Manasseh as each of full tribal status. In both instances
(as in Gen. 49) the number is twelve.

Our list, then, conserves historical, geographical and
political information of a period of Israel's history (approximately the Judges period) of which our knowledge is scanty.
Assuming, as seems most probable, a period of about 150
years from the time of the settlement to the beginning of
the monarchy, we have only the account of mainly isolated
incidents recorded in the Book of Judges. It is not surprising that we cannot more accurately relate the material
contained in this chapter. Yet, important though the historical material is, that was not the purpose in mind when
it was included in Genesis. We are being told that the events
of later days, the dispositions and relationships of the tribes,
their relative strength and weakness, are all in the mind
and purpose of God. The mighty act of salvation in Egypt
and the entry into Canaan are not the beginning of the
divine purpose for Israel. They are a fulfilment of a purpose implicit in the call of the patriarchs. We are to see the
totality of the sacral community, the people of God, in
relation to the land of Promise and in relation to the ongoing history of Canaan. The divine purpose is to be
realized in the midst of human history.

**1.** is the Priestly introduction in prose to the poetic intro-
ductory words of v. 2. It is unfortunate that AV presents

this chapter as though it were all prose. RV and RSV rightly present vv. 2-27 in poetic form, and so enable the reader to appreciate the parallelism which is so striking a feature of Hebrew poetry. IN THE LAST DAYS. Although this term is used in the prophetic literature in an eschatological sense (cf. Isa. 2.2), its meaning here is relative, yet rather more concrete than 'in the future'; we should probably understand it as 'in the culmination of those events beginning in Egypt and ending in the settlement in Canaan' So in Num. 24.14 the same phrase refers to the conquest of Moab and Edom by David.

### 3 f. Reuben.

Though the eldest of the sons he is to be unimportant. Historically, it would appear, the Reubenites settled early east of the Dead Sea and were a strong tribe. But constant wars with the Moabites reduced them to insignificance by the time of David. It is vigorously satirized in the Song of Deborah (Judg. 5.15b, 16, 'Why do you tarry among the sheep folds, to hear the piping of the flocks. Among the clans of Reuben there were great searchings of heart', RSV). Later in the monarchy period its territory became part of Moab. EXCELLENCY OF. Render 'pre-eminent in'.

### 4. thou shalt not excel

Render 'thou shalt not have the pre-eminence'. This verse refers to 35.22.

### 5-7. Simeon

and LEVI (cf. ch. 34). These two warlike yet treacherous clans lost the territory they had conquered and were scattered throughout the other tribes. This they deserved for their violation of a covenant, wherefore they were excluded from the sacral community. Historically the fate of Simeon is easier to follow; it was situated in the south of Canaan and its territory was absorbed into Judah (cf. Josh. 19.1-9 with Josh. 15.26-32, 42.) In Deut. 33 no reference is made to

Simeon. The fact that it is not called on in Judg. 5 may be
due to the fact that it was too far to the south with Judah.
The reference to Levi is more difficult. Elements of this
tribe were to be found in Egypt, and Moses was of Levitical
stock. But the curse pronounced upon Levi no less than his
character makes it very difficult to understand the high
honour associated with the name in the later life of Israel.
It is possible that there has been some confusion between
the tribal name and the professional title Levi—priest.
The tribe of Levi was, like that of Simeon, dispersed, and
disappeared as an entity. The professional levites naturally
had no specific territory except by their residence at the
sanctuaries. Whatever be the correct explanation the connection between the tribe and the priesthood is quite unknown in this chapter.

**5b.** Render ' weapons of violence are their swords '.

**6. secret**
   The word means a council of intimate friends, so render
' council '. HONOUR. The consonants could be read as ' liver '
considered as a centre of psychic energy, hence RSV
' spirit ' (cf. Ps. 16.9). DIGGED DOWN A WALL. Render
' maimed oxen '.

**7.** The curse on these tribes corresponded to the historical
facts.

**8-12. Judah**
   It is unfortunate that this blessing is in some of its details
(especially v. 10c) most obscure. In general it celebrated the
pre-eminent position of Judah, its vigour and its security.
By contrast with 37.5-10, and even 48.5, 20, Judah shall be
the most honoured tribe and the acknowledged leader. This
would seem to reflect the conditions under David.

**8.** Contains a word play that cannot be reproduced in
English, Judah (*yehudah*) they shall praise thee (*yoduka*),

thy hand (*yadka*). The terms in v. 9 express vigour and strength (AV OLD LION is in Hebrew simply another word for lion and does not suggest 'old'; RSV renders 'lioness').

## 10. lawgiver

Render 'commander's staff' (so also Num. 21.18; Ps. 60.7; 108.8). UNTIL SHILOH COME. This is one of the most puzzling phrases in Genesis; neither the ancient translations nor modern commentators are agreed about its translation or meaning. AV and RV clearly understand Shiloh to be a personal name. RV m(l), 'Till he comes to Shiloh', regards it as the sanctuary of that name (but the famous sanctuary was apparently destroyed in about 1050 BC); RSV, 'until he comes to whom it belongs', following some ancient versions, attaches different vowels and gives it a messianic character; i.e. Sovereignty shall not depart from Judah until it is manifested in David or the Messiah, son of David. A messianic significance was attached to this phrase in rabbinical circles (cf. Talmud Sanhedrin 98b) and they in turn influenced early Christian commentators. Other renderings based on emendations have been suggested: 'his ruler', 'his asked-for one', 'the peaceful one'. It should be noted that no use is made of this text in NT, and that strengthens the argument that the text in Genesis had originally no specifically messianic meaning. It is part of a general picture of Judaean superiority.

**11.** Describes a condition of abounding luxury and security, such that an ass would be allowed to browse on grapevines and wine was used for washing! The hyperbole is the more extreme in that it looks for a transformation of Judaean territory into a veritable Paradise. It would seem that the language of this whole section provided material for later messianic prophecies. (J. Lindblom, 'The Political Background of the Shiloh Oracle', *Vetus Testamentum*, Supp. I, pp. 78-87, presents a persuasive case for regarding this 'Blessing of Jacob' as a prophetic oracle, uttered dur-

ing the reign of David at Hebron (II Sam. 1-4) in preparation for his work of uniting the tribes. Shiloh is thus a
representative name for the Northern tribes. So translate
'Until he come to Shiloh').

## 13. Zebulun

In this list the order ISSACHAR-ZEBULUN is reversed (so also
Judg. 5.14 f. and Deut. 33.18). Its geographical location on
the Phoenician coast differs from that of Josh. 19.10 ff.
but resembles that of Deut. 33.19. This suggests a fluctua-
tion in the fortunes of the tribe. At the time of the oracle
the tribe is apparently engaged in maritime commerce (cf.
Deut. 33.19).

## 14 f. Issachar.

These verses are epigrammatic in character and refer to
that tribe's loss of independence and its state of vassalage.
Originally a mountain people, and heroic in defence of the
tribal confederacy (Judg. 5.15), it subsequently settled in
the plains and became subservient to the Canaanites.
STRONG, lit. 'bony'. TRIBUTE. More correctly 'forced
labour'. The passage contains a subtle allusion to the
meaning attached to the name: 'hired man' (cf. 30.17 f.).

## 16-18. Dan

The first two verses are two distinct epigrams. It begins
with a pun: *Dan yadin*—DAN SHALL JUDGE. The work of a
judge was to establish or restore the right. V. 16 would
then mean that this tribe would gain (or regain) its independence against opposition. V. 17 may well refer to the surprise attack on Laish (Judg. 18.27 f.). This tribe originally
settled on the borders of Judah, but could not maintain
their position under Philistine pressure. Their migration
northward is described in Judg. 18, which must precede
in time Judg. 5.17. V. 18 is a liturgical utterance having no
obvious connection with the material or the mood of the
blessing.

## 19. Gad

Also epigrammatic and full of word play. It opens: *gad gedud yegudennu*, which could only be reproduced in English if the tribe's name were *R*ad, then: 'Raiders shall raid Rad, but he shall raid at their heels'. GAD was a district east of the Jordan, constantly suffering from desert raiders and border warfare. It is referred to as Gilead in Judg. 5.17.

## 20. Asher

Render 'As for Asher, rich is his food' an epigram appropriate to 'fortunate' (30.13) Asher, situated in western Galilee (cf. Deut. 33.24).

## 21. Naphtali

Situated west and north of Gennesareth in a fertile district. The closing words can hardly be interpreted with certainty. A possible translation would be: 'that bears branched antlers'. This accords well with the former clause, but its further significance is not clear.

## 22-28. Joseph

This whole section is difficult of translation, and the text has clearly suffered in transmission. The general meaning is that the Joseph tribes have settled in a fruitful district, and by God-given power have been able to resist attacks. The greatest blessing of prosperity is given to him. The past tense of vv. 23 f. makes it clear that the references are to the history of this people after the settlement, as they consolidated their position in Canaan (cf. Judg. 6 f.).

## 24.

Render: 'His bow stayed firm and his arms were agile'. An echo of this appears in Ps. 78.9. Then follows a gathering together of ancient divine names: 'by the name of THE SHEPHERD, THE STONE (of Bethel) OF ISRAEL, by El of thy father . . . and El Shaddai . . .' This leads to the blessing which is so great as to extend to heaven above and to the vast cosmic deep upon which the earth was fixed (the DEEP

is the same word as in Gen. 1.2, from which the springs and
rivers were thought to come).

**26.** Render with RSV, following LXX: ' The blessings of
your father are mighty beyond the blessings of the eternal
mountains, the bounties of the everlasting hills '. SEPARATE
i.e. to cultic service, for in the Josephite territory the most
important cult centres (Gilgal, Bethel, Shiloh) were situated.
It is the word commonly translated Nazirite.

### 27. Benjamin shall ravin as a wolf

Another epigram descriptive of this war-like tribe (cf.
Judg. 20.16). Saul of this tribe made the first effective attack
on the Philistines.

**29-33.** The closing verses (P) tell of Jacob's death and his
command that he be buried in the family sepulchre. It is
stated carefully and precisely. The reason is that this field
is, in the thought of the Priestly writer, the one parcel of
land which legally belongs to Israel at this stage. It is something more than a family sepulchre; it is the earnest of
an inheritance for which the only assurance is the divine
promise. Furthermore, Israel is now in Egypt, further than
ever from realizing the promise than were Abraham and
Isaac. When moreover these words are related to the exiled
community among whom they were read and recorded, they
are seen in their true context. In the exile there were those
who had an assured hope of a return, and preserved these
stories to re-quicken the faith of the people of God.


## THE LAST ACTS OF JOSEPH

### Ch. 50

This closing chapter presents in story form the main
themes that have been stated so powerfully already; they

are now drawn together: confidence in the fulfilment of the divine promise (cf. v. 24), a re-affirmation of the Rule of God, even in the midst of human evil (v. 20), and the necessity for man's loyal obedience. It is of course not the end, except in a very limited sense. It is the necessary prelude to that mighty act of salvation which is the theme of Exodus, upon which the whole life of Israel was based. A salvation has been effected; the Salvation is yet to come. Yet there is an integral relationship between the lesser and the greater; they are both the consequences of the mighty works of God. Ancient Israel saw this re-enacted in the release from the Babylonian Exile. The Christian sees it come to its fulfilment in the death and resurrection of Christ, to which the words of v. 20 are singularly appropriate.

**1-14.** *The Burial of Jacob.* This is described with great particularity and suggests considerable knowledge of Egyptian burial customs. Embalming was not an Israelite practice, but characteristically Egyptian. The Israelite attitude to death, at least in the teaching of the OT, was extraordinarily free from morbidity. On the one hand death came for the man of God at the time appointed by God; on the other he lived on in the family of the people of God. Of course they mourned the death of those they loved; but they were forbidden to indulge in extravagant sorrow. When, at the end of the OT, Israel came to a hope for life beyond this, it was based, not on the ritual preparation of the corpse, but on the good will of God toward those whom he had already made his own. Embalming was a practice foreign to Israel, and practised here in order to convey Jacob to the family grave.

### 3. Threescore and ten days

Corresponds to the length of time for a royal mourning in Egypt, viz. 72 days.

**4.** Probably Joseph, in a state of ritual mourning, could not come personally into the presence of Pharaoh, but would need to have royal permission to leave the country.

**5.** Suggests a grave other than the cave of Machpelah and this is supported by vv. 10, 11, which speak of some district east of Jordan. It is possible that there is preserved here a fragment of an old tradition which associated Jacob's tomb with a place in this district.

**7-9.** It is at least probable that the considerable Egyptian bodyguard was as much to ensure the return of Joseph and his brother, as to do them honour; so the families and possessions remain in Goshen as a pledge of good faith.

**10.** To get to Transjordan they would pass close to the cave of MACHPELAH. ATAD—thornbush, cf. Judg. 9.14 f. ('bramble').

**11. Abel**
means 'watercourse'; MOURNING is in Hebrew *'ēbel*. On the part of the Egyptians this would be a conventional mourning. Jacob was given honourable burial.

**12 f.** Comes from the Priestly sources and so continues the tradition of 25.9; 35.27-29; 49.29-33.

**15-26.** *The end of the Joseph Story.* This is told with remarkable realism and acute understanding of human nature. The profound generosity of Joseph and his unreserved forgiveness of his brothers has not fully reached his brothers. They are still suffering from the evil they have done, and so inevitably they judge him by their own standards. He might well have refrained from reprisals while the father was alive, but now there are no restraints. They suffer for fear of what may happen to them. Joseph is distressed on their behalf. This leads to the full reconciliation, not merely on the ground of brotherly love, but on the basis of the sovereign purpose of God (v. 20).

**19.** God has proved his good purpose for them. For Joseph to act in any other way would be to set himself in opposition to God, and so to set himself up as another god. He, as the loyal man of God, can only act in a way consistent with the revealed (through the events) will of God.

**20.** This is the focal point of the whole Joseph story. The verbs in AV, THOUGHT, MEANT are the same word in Hebrew, 'you planned . . . God planned', indicating the total movement of the personality towards the action. The active purpose of God was at work even through the evil purpose of the brothers.

**21.** This gives the final word of reconciliation, which Joseph 'spoke upon their heart' (AV, SPAKE KINDLY); i.e. the word charged with the whole personality or soul of Joseph came upon the innermost source of their life to make them at one with him.

**22.** The age of 110 was regarded in Egypt as the extreme limit of human life.

**23.** Presents this in more distinctively Israelite terms, not so much as a number of years but as the fulfilment of the good life (cf. Job 42.16).

**24-26.** The closing words of the book are both an end and a beginning, a reiteration of the promise, and a preparation for its fulfilment. That is the point that is made in Heb. 11.22: 'By faith' . . . 'the faith that gives substance to our hopes and makes us certain of realities we do not see' (Heb. 11.1 N.E.B.).